Engaged Empathy Leadership

Engaged Empathy Leadership

Redefining Leadership with Empathy in Action

Jeff LeBlanc, DBA

BEP
BUSINESS EXPERT PRESS
Leader in applied, concise business books

First published in 2025 by
Business Expert Press, LLC
222 East 46th Street, New York, NY 10017
www.businessexpertpress.com

ISBN-13: 978-1-63742-878-8 (paperback)
ISBN-13: 978-1-63742-879-5 (e-book)

Human Resource Management and Organizational Behavior Collection

First edition: 2025

10 9 8 7 6 5 4 3 2 1

EU SAFETY REPRESENTATIVE
Mare Nostrum Group B.V.
Mauritskade 21D
1091 GC Amsterdam
The Netherlands
gpsr@mare-nostrum.co.uk

To my family—thank you for the love, laughter, and guidance. I'll love you forever and ever, amen.

To Bo, my loyal friend—I hope heaven has endless treats, open fields, and no nail trimmings.

To my students—you sparked this journey with your questions, your honesty, and your belief that leadership could (and should) be better.

And to all the leaders I've met—both the inspiring and the insufferable—thank you. You showed me who I want to be...and who I absolutely don't.

Description

Leadership isn't just about understanding people—it's about actively engaging with them to build trust, achieve results, and cultivate sustainable success. Engaged Empathy Leadership Model (EELM) introduces a groundbreaking approach that moves beyond passive empathy, creating workplaces where employees feel genuinely valued, challenged, and empowered. Rooted in extensive research, real-world case studies, and deep insights into Generation Z workplace expectations, EELM provides a practical framework built on three essential pillars: kindness, fairness, and structure. Leaders who embrace these principles don't just enhance workplace culture; they significantly improve employee retention, productivity, and overall organizational engagement.

This book guides leaders, managers, and HR (human resources) professionals in transforming empathy from passive understanding into decisive, accountable action. You'll learn to cultivate a fair workplace that builds genuine trust, implement structured leadership strategies to clearly outline expectations and career paths, and effectively motivate employees through active empathy that maintains performance standards. Whether you're managing a startup team or leading a multinational corporation, Engaged Empathy Leadership Model equips you with the tools to bridge generational divides, foster a culture of accountability, and retain top talent. Now is the moment to evolve your leadership approach—moving from passive empathy to engaged empathy—and create workplaces where employees thrive, innovate, and commit for the long term.

Table of Contents

List of Figures

Review Quote

"*The* Engaged Empathy Leadership *model resonates deeply with me as an early career talent expert who has seen multiple generations navigate the workforce over the past couple of decades. It represents what's truly needed as workplaces evolve—giving voice and direction to the future of work. Gen Z is demanding the same fairness, collaboration, and balance that prior generations wanted but were perhaps hesitant to ask for. This model brings structure to that movement, making it an essential leadership framework for today's workforce.*"—**Suzanne Rosenthal, HR Talent Executive and Former VP of Campus & Early Career Talent at Paramount**

Introduction

Engaged Empathy Leadership Model™

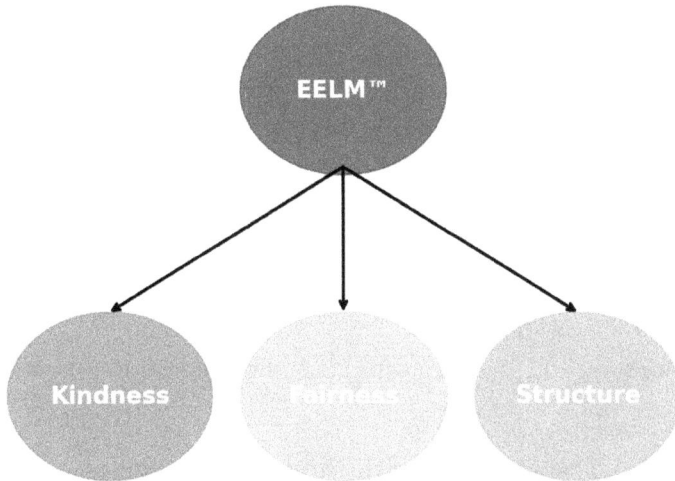

Figure 1: Engaged Empathy Leadership Model

Empathy without action is just a feeling. Leadership requires movement. The Engaged Empathy Leadership Model drives real business impact by turning understanding into action—powered by its three pillars: kindness, fairness, and structure.

—Jeff LeBlanc, DBA

Why Traditional Leadership Models No Longer Work

Leadership is broken. Not because people aren't trying—but because they're still clinging to dusty, outdated ideas of what leadership *should* look like.

For years, the message has been clear: Empathy is the answer. Be more understanding. Listen more. Create a supportive culture. And yes, those things matter. But here's the hard truth—empathy alone doesn't move the needle.

If it did, every manager who held open-door hours, asked about weekends, and handed out the occasional "You're doing great" would be leading a dream team. But that's not what we're seeing. Instead, even well-meaning, people-focused leaders are grappling with burnout, disengagement, and teams that feel more disconnected than ever.

Why? Because passive empathy isn't leadership—it's just polite observation. It's like standing on the shore telling someone you hope they make it across, when what they need is a boat, a paddle, and someone willing to row alongside them.

Leadership requires more than heart. It requires action, clarity, and the courage to hold people capable—not just comfortable.

Leadership isn't about feeling for people. It's about engaging with them in a way that turns understanding into action. It's about creating a workplace where employees aren't just heard but rather empowered, supported, and held accountable.

That's where Engaged Empathy Leadership Model (EELM) comes in.

The Problem with Modern Leadership

Leaders today face an impossible balance. They are told to be kind but not be a pushover, to be approachable but maintain authority, to be flexible but also set clear expectations. As a result, many default to one of two extremes:

1. The Overempathizer—This leader believes that good leadership means prioritizing employee happiness above all else. They listen, accommodate, and avoid hard conversations. They operate under the philosophy that if employees feel supported, they will perform well. But, in reality, a lack of structure and accountability leads to unclear expectations, frustration, and even disengagement. Employees may like this leader, but they don't necessarily respect them. This is a flaw often seen in servant leadership, where the desire to serve employees can sometimes come at the expense of setting a firm direction.

2. The Detached Decision Maker—This leader focuses purely on performance, policies, and measurable results but fails to connect

with their people. Employees may know exactly what is expected of them, but they don't trust leadership because they feel like numbers rather than individuals. This is common in transactional leadership, which emphasizes structure and rewards but neglects personal engagement. While this approach can create efficiency, it rarely fosters long-term motivation or loyalty.

Neither approach works. Leaders who are too soft lose authority. Leaders who are too rigid lose engagement.

Servant leadership, while valuable in many ways, can sometimes overprioritize individual employee needs at the expense of the organization's long-term strategy. Transactional leadership, on the other hand, ensures structure and consistency but can make employees feel interchangeable.

The best leaders find a balance. They don't just care about their employees—they create an environment where employees can succeed, feel valued, and know exactly what's expected of them.

That's what Engaged Empathy Leadership Model does—it bridges the gap between being empathetic and being effective.

What Is Engaged Empathy Leadership Model (EELM)?

EELM is built on three essential pillars that every great leader must master:

- Kindness: Not just "being nice" but actively engaging with employees in a way that builds trust and psychological safety. Leaders who practice kindness create workplaces where employees feel seen and valued—without sacrificing accountability.
- Fairness: Employees don't need to agree with every decision, but they need to understand how and why those decisions are made. Transparent leadership builds trust. Misleading employees—intentionally or not—destroys it.
- Structure: People don't thrive in chaos. Leadership must provide clear expectations, structured feedback, and defined pathways for growth. Without structure, even the most well-intentioned leadership efforts fall apart.

When Kindness, Fairness, and Structure work together, employees don't just feel good at work—they perform at their best.

EELM ensures that leadership is engaged, empathetic, and effective. It provides the human connection missing from transactional leadership and the accountability often lacking in servant leadership. It creates leaders who don't just listen but act—who don't just support but empower.

That's the difference. And that's why leadership needs to change.

Why This Book Matters Now

Leadership is at a crossroads. Traditional management approaches are losing effectiveness, workplace expectations are rapidly evolving, and employees—especially Gen Z—are demanding more from their leaders than ever before. At the same time, leaders are struggling to adapt to a workforce that is more vocal, more purpose-driven, and less tolerant of outdated hierarchies and rigid corporate structures.

Many organizations still rely on outdated leadership models that no longer align with the way people work today. Transactional leadership, with its focus on rewards and punishments, creates short-term compliance but fails to foster long-term loyalty or innovation. Servant leadership, while well intentioned, often lacks the structure needed to ensure fairness, accountability, and clear decision making. And in some workplaces, leaders have leaned so far into emotional intelligence and support that they avoid making tough decisions, setting boundaries, or maintaining performance expectations.

The result? High turnover, disengaged employees, and leaders who feel stuck—trying to be everything to everyone but never quite getting it right.

This book isn't another "feel-good leadership" guide filled with vague inspiration or generic advice. It's a practical, research-backed framework built from real-world case studies, data-driven insights, and firsthand experience working with leaders across industries. It offers a leadership model that actually works—one that balances empathy with action, human connection with accountability, and flexibility with structure.

What You'll Gain from This Book

- Give feedback that actually helps employees grow—Learn how to deliver constructive feedback that drives improvement without triggering defensiveness or disengagement.
- Create a culture of value and accountability—Strike the balance between making employees feel valued while ensuring they own their responsibilities and results.
- Make promotions, raises, and opportunities truly fair— Understand how to structure leadership decisions based on equity and performance—not just who speaks the loudest or has the best personal connections.
- Lead in a way that retains top talent—Develop leadership strategies that engage, motivate, and keep high-performing Gen Z and millennial employees invested in their work.
- Bridge generational leadership gaps—Effectively lead a workforce that includes baby boomers, Gen X, millennials, and Gen Z—each with different workplace expectations, motivations, and communication styles.

Why Now?

- Retention is a crisis. Companies aren't just losing employees due to salary concerns—they're losing them because of poor leadership, unclear expectations, and workplace cultures that don't provide growth or fairness.
- Gen Z is changing the rules. This generation expects more than just a paycheck. They want purpose, flexibility, transparency, and real leadership—not just an open-door policy or a friendly boss.
- Leaders are feeling lost. Many managers and executives weren't trained for this shift and are struggling to find a leadership style that resonates with today's workforce.
- The future of leadership depends on adaptation. Leaders who fail to evolve will continue losing their best employees, while those who adapt will create engaged, high-performing teams that thrive.

This book is for leaders who are done playing catch-up—leaders who want a clear, effective strategy for leading with confidence, clarity, and fairness.

Leadership isn't just about understanding employees—it's about engaging with them in a way that drives action, trust, and results.

It's time to evolve leadership for the modern workplace.

What Leaders Get Wrong About Gen Z (And How EELM Fixes It)

Gen Z isn't the prevailing problem. Leadership models that don't adapt are the major problem.

For years, leaders have blamed younger employees for being impatient, demanding, or resistant to traditional workplace norms. But my research shows that Gen Z employees aren't rejecting leadership—they're redefining it. They aren't disengaged because they don't want to work hard. They're disengaged because leadership is failing to provide what they need to succeed.

Through my research—including surveys of Gen Z employees across industries like technology, education, manufacturing, and hospitality—I found that Gen Z workers aren't simply seeking perks or flexibility. They are looking for leadership that is transparent, structured, and actively engaged in their success.

What Gen Z Actually Wants from Leadership

- Clarity—No vague expectations. They want to know exactly what success looks like. Eighty-seven percent of Gen Z employees in my study preferred structured performance reviews and defined career paths over informal evaluations. They don't want to be left guessing about how to grow in their roles.
- Transparency—No empty reassurances. They want to know how decisions are made, whether it's about promotions, raises, or organizational changes. Sixty-seven percent of Gen Z employees said they are more likely to stay at a company long-term if leadership is clear about how career growth works.

- Engagement—No passive leadership. They want leaders who actively help them grow. Eighty-five percent of Gen Z employees agreed that empathy in leadership improves workplace culture, but they also said that empathy without fairness and structure feels hollow. They don't just want a boss who listens—they want a leader who takes action.

These preferences aren't unreasonable. They reflect a workforce that values trust, fairness, and career development over outdated workplace traditions.

Leadership today isn't about demanding respect based on hierarchy—it's about earning trust through action.

Gen Z isn't asking for leadership to be easier. They're asking for leadership to be better.

A Leadership Model That Actually Works

The best leaders don't choose between results and relationships—they know that the two are inseparable. Engaged Empathy Leadership Model (EELM) is built on the idea that you don't have to sacrifice one for the other. A strong workplace culture and high performance are not competing goals; they reinforce each other.

Too many leadership models force leaders into a false choice:

- Do you focus on employee well-being at the expense of performance?
- Do you push for results but risk alienating your team?
- Do you become a hands-off leader and hope your team figures it out on their own?

None of these approaches work long-term. Leaders who fail to engage with their employees lose trust. Leaders who fail to provide structure create confusion and disengagement. And leaders who avoid accountability end up with teams that underperform or leave altogether.

EELM ensures that leaders don't just manage employees—they engage them, empower them, and set them up to succeed.

EELM helps a leader:

- Retain top talent instead of losing them to competitors: Employees don't leave jobs; they leave leaders. They leave when they don't see fairness, career growth, or meaningful engagement. EELM helps you build an environment where employees want to stay—not just for the paycheck but for the leadership that helps them thrive.
- Build high-performing teams that actually trust you: Trust isn't built on friendliness alone. Employees trust leaders who are transparent, set clear expectations, and follow through on commitments. EELM provides a framework that strengthens that trust through consistent actions, not just words.
- Create a work environment where people want to stay, grow, and contribute: Culture isn't about free snacks or flexible schedules. It's about how people feel when they show up to work every day. Do they feel valued? Do they feel like their efforts matter? Do they know what success looks like? EELM ensures that leadership isn't reactive—it's intentional, structured, and designed to keep employees engaged.

Leadership isn't about maintaining a title or checking off a list of responsibilities. It's about creating a workplace where people don't just work—they perform, grow, and commit.

If you're ready to lead in a way that gets results and earns trust, then let's get started.

A Note to Skeptical Leaders

If you're reading this thinking, *Great, another trendy leadership model that will be outdated in 5 years,* I understand.

The workplace has been flooded with new leadership philosophies, each claiming to be the solution to all of today's challenges. Some come and go, driven by fleeting corporate trends. But Engaged Empathy Leadership Model (EELM) isn't a trend—it's a necessary shift in how leadership needs to evolve.

This isn't about discarding the past or minimizing what previous generations of leaders have accomplished. The challenges leaders face today are different from those of the past, just as today's workforce is different from the one that came before it. What worked in an era of strict hierarchy, long tenure, and clearly defined career ladders doesn't necessarily apply in a world where employees expect transparency, flexibility, and a sense of purpose in their work.

But that doesn't mean one generation is right and another is wrong. This is not an "us versus them" scenario. This isn't about younger workers rejecting leadership or older leaders being "out of touch." It's about recognizing that leadership must evolve, just as it always has.

Think about it—leadership has never been static. The way businesses operated in the 1950s was different from the 1980s, which was different from the 2000s. The best leaders didn't resist change—rather, they adapted. They learned from those before them, improved where necessary, and built something stronger for the future. That's what EELM is all about.

The old models—authoritative leadership, passive empathy, or rigid hierarchical decision making—weren't built for today's workforce. And the companies that don't adapt? They're the ones struggling with high turnover, low engagement, and frustrated teams.

But the organizations that embrace this shift will thrive.

This book isn't about discarding the past—it's about building on what works, fixing what doesn't, and creating a leadership model that serves both employees and organizations in a lasting way.

No matter where you are in your leadership journey, there's room to grow. We can all learn from each other—leaders from different generations, industries, and experiences—because the goal is the same: to create workplaces where people perform at their best and leadership truly works.

PART 1

The Problem—Where Leadership Falls Short

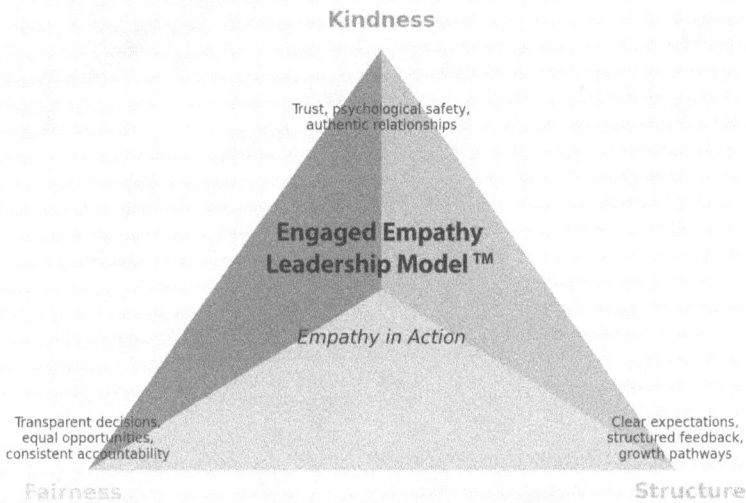

Kindness

Trust, psychological safety, authentic relationships

Engaged Empathy Leadership Model ™

Empathy in Action

Transparent decisions, equal opportunities, consistent accountability

Clear expectations, structured feedback, growth pathways

Fairness

Structure

Figure 2: Engaged Empathy Leadership

CHAPTER 1

The Misconception of Empathy in Leadership

Why Leaders Think They're Being Empathetic But Aren't

Most leaders believe they're empathetic. They pride themselves on being approachable, on listening, on fostering an open and friendly work culture. They say the right things, nod in meetings, celebrate birthdays, and send the occasional "Hope you're doing well" e-mail.

And yet, when employees leave their jobs, the most common reason they cite isn't salary, benefits, or workload—it's leadership.

This disconnect between leaders' perception of their own empathy and the reality of how their employees experience them is one of the most overlooked failures in leadership today. Leaders think they're being empathetic because they're nice. But there's a fundamental difference between being nice and being kind—a difference that shapes how employees feel supported, valued, and motivated in their roles.

Nice is easy. Nice is surface level. Nice is pleasantries, small talk, and a well-placed smile.

Kindness, that's work.

I've known plenty of nice people who weren't kind in the least, and I've met plenty of people who came across as mean but were some of the kindest individuals I've ever known. I learned this lesson firsthand from two teachers I had in high school—one whom everyone hated and the other whom everyone loved.

The Nice Teacher Versus The Kind Teacher

The first teacher was the toughest instructor I ever had. She was sharp, blunt, and never sugarcoated anything. She didn't relate to students, didn't try to be our friend, and certainly didn't make class "fun." Her classroom was strict, her grading harsh, and her expectations clear.

But you know what she did do? She stayed after school every other day with students like me, making sure we understood the material and could succeed. She held us accountable, challenged us, and invested her time in making sure we performed to the best of our abilities. She didn't offer empty encouragement—she offered real support, the kind that made a difference.

That's kindness.

She never once called herself kind—she didn't need to. Because kindness isn't a label you put on yourself. It's something other people recognize in you.

On the other hand, there was another teacher—Mr. Cool. Everyone loved him. He cracked jokes, related to students, and was the kind of teacher you looked forward to seeing in the hallway. He made people feel good—until they needed something from him.

Fail a test? Suddenly, you weren't on his radar. Need extra help? He'd cancel after-school hours to catch a game or hang out at football practice. He made students feel seen when it was convenient, but when it mattered most, he was nowhere to be found. He was the nicest asshole I'd ever met.

The difference between these two teachers is the same difference we see in leadership today.

The Consequences of Mistaking Niceness for Kindness

The distinction between kindness and niceness isn't just a personal observation—it has real consequences in leadership. When leaders mistake surface-level empathy for real engagement, they unknowingly create a workplace where problems fester beneath the surface. Employees feel unheard. Growth stalls. Resentment builds. And over time, the result is burnout, favoritism, and emotional labor overload—three silent killers of workplace culture and performance.

But here's the catch: The problem isn't that leaders don't care. Most do.

The problem is that many leaders confuse performative empathy with engaged empathy.

They think that if they're friendly and available, they're doing enough. They assume that if their employees like them, they must be leading well. They believe that as long as they maintain a positive atmosphere, their team will thrive.

But real leadership—the kind that *earns trust and drives impact*—requires *action*, not just intent.

Engaged Empathy Versus Performative Empathy

Being an empathetic leader *isn't* about being everyone's friend. It's about showing up when it matters—having the hard conversations, making tough but fair decisions, and ensuring people have what they need to succeed.

It's about holding people accountable while supporting them at the same time.

It's about being the kind of leader who might not always be liked in the moment—but who, years later, employees will look back on and say, "They were tough, but damn, they cared."

That's the difference between surface-level empathy *and* engaged empathy. And that's where leadership often falls short.

In most workplaces today, leadership feels like a tightrope act, swinging dangerously between two extremes—leaders either lean too far into empathy, prioritizing likability at the expense of accountability, or they rigidly cling to structure, sacrificing genuine human connection for results-driven metrics alone. Traditional leadership styles, whether the warmth-heavy servant leader who hesitates to deliver tough feedback or the transactional boss who views employees as interchangeable cogs, often unintentionally fuel burnout, disengagement, or resentment. Engaged Empathy Leadership Model (EELM), however, offers a third path, rejecting the notion that kindness and accountability are mutually exclusive. It insists that empathy must move beyond passive understanding to active engagement, balancing genuine care with fairness and clear expectations. In doing so, EELM transforms workplaces from places of surface-level positivity or rigid bureaucracy into environments where employees feel not only valued but motivated, where leadership isn't just a title but an ongoing commitment to meaningful action, trust, and growth.

Servant Leadership	EELM™
Focuses on putting employees' needs first and fostering a strong culture of support.	Focuses on balancing empathy with structured leadership to ensure fairness and business results.
Encourages leaders to act as servants to their teams.	Encourages leaders to act as partners in engagement, providing clear guidance while supporting employees.
Can create leadership burnout if leaders overextend themselves.	Prevents burnout by ensuring leaders maintain authority and structure.
Sometimes lacks clear guidelines on accountability and expectations.	Establishes structured feedback systems to keep both leaders and employees accountable.

Figure 3: Comparison between Servant Leadership and EELM

Transactional Leadership	EELM™
Focuses on strict hierarchy, rules, and reward systems.	Provides clear structure without rigidity, balancing accountability with flexibility.
Employees receive rewards or punishments based on performance metrics.	Employees receive fair, structured feedback and transparent career paths.
Lacks empathy—prioritizes efficiency over engagement.	Prioritizes engagement without sacrificing structure and business goals.
Can feel rigid, bureaucratic, and outdated for modern employees.	Appeals to modern employees (especially Gen Z) by integrating structure with fairness and engagement.

Figure 4: Comparison between Transactional Leadership and EELM

Rethinking "Soft" Skills: The Hardest Leadership Challenge

For too long, we've referred to empathy, communication, adaptability, and emotional intelligence as *soft* skills, as if they are secondary to technical expertise or operational efficiency. The term itself—*soft*—implies that these skills are easy, optional, or less valuable than so-called hard skills like data analysis, financial modeling, or strategic planning.

This is a dangerous and outdated mindset.

In reality, the ability to connect, lead with empathy, and navigate human relationships in the workplace is often far more difficult than learning technical skills. Managing spreadsheets or mastering a software program can be taught in a matter of weeks. Learning how to have tough conversations, give constructive feedback, build trust, and create an inclusive workplace? That takes years of practice, experience, and self-awareness.

These so-called soft skills are actually the hardest and most essential leadership skills. They determine:

- Whether employees trust their leaders enough to stay.
- Whether teams work together effectively or fall into dysfunction.
- Whether an organization can navigate change, resolve conflict, and create a workplace culture that attracts top talent.

The Engaged Empathy Leadership Model (EELM) refines and strengthens these critical skills. It doesn't treat empathy, fairness, and structure as abstract ideals—it gives leaders a clear framework to develop, implement, and sustain these skills in their organizations.

Leaders need to stop seeing *soft* skills as a luxury or a secondary focus. They are the core of effective leadership. If organizations continue to undervalue them, they will struggle to lead in a world where empathy, fairness, and structure are nonnegotiable expectations—especially for Gen Z employees.

The challenge isn't whether to invest in these skills—the challenge is whether leaders are willing to acknowledge that they are just as demanding, measurable, and essential as any technical skill in business. And perhaps even harder to master.

The Risks of Passive Empathy: Burnout, Favoritism, and Emotional Labor Overload

Smiles don't pay the bills—though wouldn't it be nice if they could?

If leadership were as easy as nodding with conviction, listening with empathy, and flashing your best "I understand" grin, every workplace would be a utopia of engaged teams and soaring profits. But as anyone who's managed people knows, empathy without action might earn you fans—but it won't keep your lights on, your best talent around, or your business thriving.

A smile is easy. It takes no effort to plaster on a grin and offer pleasantries during a meeting or a performance review. But building trust, making tough decisions, and having difficult conversations? That's hard.

Real empathy demands courage—the willingness to step into uncomfortable territory, to acknowledge struggles openly, and to prioritize honesty over harmony. Empathy isn't just warmth; it's strength in vulnerability, clarity in confusion, and conviction amid uncertainty. Anyone can smile, but true leaders pair that warmth with substance. They recognize that compassion without accountability is hollow—and that the strongest teams are built not on polite smiles alone, but on the sturdy foundation of trust, candor, and consistent follow-through.

This is exactly why soft skills aren't actually soft—they're some of the hardest to master. A smile can make an employee feel momentarily welcome, but it won't:

- Clarify expectations when they're confused about their role.
- Hold people accountable when performance is slipping.
- Build a culture of fairness where employees know promotions and raises aren't based on favoritism.
- Encourage someone to stay when they're debating leaving for a competitor.

Leadership requires more than surface-level gestures. Employees don't need leaders who just make them feel good in the moment—they need leaders who create an environment where they feel valued, challenged, and supported in the long run.

Smiling at your team is nice. But leading them with engaged empathy—through fairness, structure, and clear expectations—is what drives success.

We all want to work in a place that feels positive, welcoming, and supportive. Leaders want to be seen as approachable and understanding. It's human nature to want to be liked, to create harmony, to make people feel good.

But there's a problem. Passive empathy—being agreeable, pleasant, and overly focused on making people feel good—creates a workplace that looks perfect on the surface but is full of cracks underneath.

It turns work into something that feels like a Norman Rockwell painting—quaint, comforting, nostalgic. It's a picture-perfect representation of what we think a workplace should be. But like Rockwell's paintings, it's a fantasy. It's not built to handle the messiness of real business, real leadership, or real people. And when passive empathy takes over, three things start happening.

Burnout: When Leaders and Employees Give Too Much Without Getting Support

Passive empathy often leads to emotional overextension—leaders feeling like they have to be everything to everyone, employees feeling like they have to be constantly agreeable, and no one setting real boundaries. In environments where empathy lacks structure, exhaustion isn't a sign of working hard; it's a sign of a system that isn't working at all.

Leaders who engage in passive empathy often:

- Say yes to everything to avoid disappointing others.
- Take on emotional burdens that should be distributed across the team.
- Struggle to have hard conversations because they don't want to upset people.
- Absorb employee stress without offering real solutions.

And employees mirror this behavior. They smile through their exhaustion, nod in agreement even when they disagree, and hesitate to speak up when they need support because they don't want to "rock the boat." The expectation isn't just to do their jobs—it's to be endlessly flexible, relentlessly positive, and always available.

Over time, this builds into burnout—not just for employees but for leaders as well. The same leaders who wanted to create a supportive, people-first culture find themselves drained, overwhelmed, and unable to maintain the very engagement they once prioritized. Employees, seeing their leaders exhausted and overextended, follow suit. Productivity declines, frustration rises, and the workplace becomes a cycle of quiet suffering, where no one feels empowered to set limits or ask for help.

Empathy should *never* come at the expense of sustainability. Real leadership means recognizing that saying yes to everything isn't kindness—it's a failure to set priorities. It means creating a culture where support is shared, where employees feel comfortable voicing concerns without fear, and where setting boundaries isn't seen as a weakness but as a necessity for long-term success.

A truly empathetic workplace isn't one where people burn themselves out for the sake of others—it's one where leaders and employees alike feel valued, supported, and empowered to do their best work without sacrificing themselves in the process.

Favoritism: When Niceness Replaces Fairness

One of the biggest dangers of passive empathy is that it rewards the loudest voices, the friendliest personalities, and the people whom leaders naturally "click" with—rather than those who truly deserve recognition. In a workplace where empathy lacks structure, decisions aren't made based on clear performance metrics or objective standards. Instead, they're shaped by personal comfort, team dynamics, and emotional connections.

That's how high-performing employees are overlooked while those who master office politics continue to rise.

It starts subtly. A leader promotes someone they feel they can trust—someone who gets along well with the team, shares their sense of humor, or knows how to make the right impression in meetings. Over time, the pattern repeats. The same employees are given promotions, high-visibility projects, and career-building opportunities, not necessarily because they are the most capable but because they know how to navigate the unspoken rules of workplace favoritism.

Meanwhile, others who deliver results but don't actively self-promote are left behind. The quiet problem solvers, the reliable contributors, the employees who do great work but aren't constantly in their boss's ear—they begin to feel invisible. Some push harder, hoping that effort alone will be recognized. Others disengage, realizing that no amount of hard work will compensate for not being one of the favorites.

Resentment takes root. Employees begin to see advancement as less about performance and more about playing the game. Trust in leadership erodes, and a toxic culture emerges—one where success depends less on what you do and more on who you know.

This kind of favoritism isn't always intentional. Most leaders don't set out to create an unfair system. But when empathy isn't balanced by fairness and structure, decisions become subjective, and merit takes a backseat to likability.

Real leadership means recognizing these biases and correcting them. It means creating clear, transparent pathways for advancement, ensuring that every employee—whether they are the most outgoing or the most reserved—has an equal shot at success. It means ensuring that empathy doesn't just extend to the people leaders naturally connect with but to everyone who works hard and delivers results.

Empathy without structure isn't leadership—its favoritism dressed up as kindness.

The Hidden Costs of Passive Empathy in Promotion Decisions

At a midsize tech company where I consulted, a department head—let's call him Mark—prided himself on being an empathetic leader. He had an open-door policy, frequently checked in on his team, and made a point of fostering a friendly, collaborative work environment. His employees appreciated his warmth, and he genuinely cared about their well-being. But when it came to promotions, his approach to leadership revealed a serious flaw.

Each year, the company promoted two employees to managerial roles. The selection process was informal, without clearly defined performance criteria. Instead of using objective measures, Mark relied on his instincts, believing he could recognize leadership potential based on how well he knew and trusted his team members.

Without realizing it, he consistently promoted employees he felt most comfortable with—those who were outgoing, vocal in meetings, and had strong personal relationships with him and other senior leaders. These individuals weren't necessarily the highest-performing employees, but they excelled at self-promotion. They made sure to be seen, to speak up, and to cultivate relationships with the right people.

At the same time, several quieter, highly competent employees who delivered excellent work were repeatedly passed over for promotions. They assumed their contributions would speak for themselves, that their dedication and results would be enough to earn recognition. But in Mark's unstructured system, where promotions were based more on perceived charisma than on measurable performance, they were consistently overlooked.

Over time, resentment began to build. Employees who had spent years delivering strong results realized that no matter how hard they worked, they would never be considered for advancement if they weren't naturally charismatic or socially engaged. Some tried to adapt by networking more aggressively, while others withdrew, feeling demotivated by a system that seemed rigged against them.

The turning point came when two of the department's top performers resigned within weeks of each other. In their exit interviews, both cited the same reason: they felt invisible. They had given everything to their roles, but when promotion decisions were made, they were never in the conversation. One departing employee put it succinctly: "If you're not one of the favorites, it doesn't matter what you do."

Mark was stunned. He had never considered himself to be playing favorites, but the feedback forced him to confront the reality of his approach. His passive empathy—his tendency to reward those he had the strongest personal connections with—had created an unfair system that valued likability over competence.

Determined to correct this, he worked with HR to introduce a structured promotion process. Clear performance metrics were established, and all employees were given a transparent roadmap for career advancement. Leadership potential was evaluated based on measurable contributions rather than personal rapport.

The changes didn't happen overnight, but over time, they restored trust in the process. Employees who had once felt sidelined began to see real pathways to advancement. Promotions became more balanced, and while strong interpersonal skills were still valued, they were no longer the primary factor in career progression.

The lesson was clear: Empathy alone isn't enough. Without fairness and structure, even well-intentioned leaders can create cultures where only the most visible and socially skilled employees thrive. True leadership requires recognizing and rewarding all forms of excellence, not just the ones that stand out in the moment.

Emotional Labor Overload: When Work Becomes More About Feelings Than Function

When passive empathy dominates a workplace, leaders and employees start carrying an unspoken emotional weight—a constant pressure to manage how others feel rather than focusing on the work itself.

- Employees feel like they have to read between the lines instead of getting clear feedback.
- Leaders spend more time managing emotions than managing outcomes.
- Workplace culture shifts from growth and accountability to walking on eggshells.

And the worst part, it makes people exhausted. Constantly monitoring how you come across, worrying about upsetting others, and filtering every conversation through an emotional lens instead of a functional one wears people down. And it distracts one from the real work that needs to be done.

The Fantasy Versus the Reality

I adore Norman Rockwell paintings—the nostalgic Thanksgiving feasts, smiling neighbors chatting over white picket fences, or rose-cheeked kids fishing off idyllic docks. They're pure Americana—dreamy scenes where problems are small and smiles solve everything. And don't get me wrong, I love a good Rockwell moment just like I love being agreeable, nodding warmly, and keeping conversations pleasant. But leadership isn't *The Saturday Evening Post* cover, and real-life challenges can't be solved by simply smiling and passing the gravy. Authentic empathy in leadership is messier, more nuanced, and far more demanding. It requires stepping beyond the frame into uncomfortable territory, where honest conversations, tough decisions, and genuine accountability create trust that lasts long after the nostalgia fades.

A workplace built on passive empathy alone looks nice—it feels warm, friendly, and positive. But scratch beneath the surface, and you'll find exhaustion, frustration, and a whole lot of hidden resentment.

If passive empathy is so destructive, why do so many leaders still fall into the trap? The answer lies in how leadership effectiveness is measured—or, more often, mismeasured. Many leaders believe they're doing enough simply because their teams seem comfortable or because no one is openly complaining. But the research tells a very different story.

That's why engaged empathy is different. It's about balancing kindness with fairness and structure—ensuring people feel supported while also holding them accountable, leading with care while making tough decisions, and recognizing that leadership isn't about making people comfortable. It's about making them better.

Research on Leadership Effectiveness and Engagement

There's no shortage of studies on leadership, but one thing is clear—leaders who balance empathy with action create the strongest, most engaged teams. The problem? Most leaders think they're already doing this, when in reality, they're often leaning too far into either passive empathy or rigid structure.

Research consistently shows that employees don't leave jobs; they leave leaders. A Gallup study found that 70 percent of the variance in employee engagement is directly tied to the quality of their manager (Gallup 2017). Yet, despite this overwhelming influence, many leaders overestimate their effectiveness.

- A 2018 McKinsey report found that 86 percent of leaders rated themselves as good listeners, but only 23 percent of employees agreed (McKinsey & Company 2018).
- *Harvard Business Review* reported that 58 percent of employees trust a stranger more than their own boss (*Harvard Business Review* 2016).
- A study by DDI found that 57 percent of employees have left a job specifically because of their manager (DDI 2019).

The disconnect isn't just about empathy versus results—it's about how leaders define engagement in the first place. Too many leaders mistake superficial harmony for genuine buy-in, thinking a smiling team is a committed team. But true engagement isn't reflected in polite nods or cheerful small talk over coffee—it's revealed in the gritty moments: when your people willingly tackle tough challenges, openly voice concerns, and trust you enough to deliver uncomfortable truths.

If leaders keep confusing Rockwellian pleasantness with authentic engagement, they'll build picture-perfect facades—but not thriving teams. Real engagement requires more than making everyone feel cozy and comfortable; it means creating an environment where honesty flourishes, trust runs deep, and the path to success isn't paved only with smiles but also with shared commitment, candor, and clarity.

Many leaders assume that if employees aren't complaining, they must be happy. That if a team is getting along, they must be engaged. That if people seem comfortable, they must be performing at their best. But comfort isn't the same as engagement.

Research shows that the best workplaces aren't built on comfort alone—they are built on purpose, challenge, and support (Dweck 2006). Employees don't just want to feel safe in their jobs; they want to feel motivated, valued, and pushed to do their best work. Without the right leadership, even a workplace that feels pleasant can stagnate, leading to low productivity, hidden disengagement, and quiet quitting (Gallup 2023).

A major study from Google's Project Oxygen sought to identify what makes a great leader. The results showed that the best managers are those who (Google 2013):

- Provide clear expectations and structure, rather than leaving employees to figure things out on their own.
- Give direct feedback, even when it's difficult, so that employees always know where they stand.
- Offer support without micromanaging, empowering employees to take ownership of their work.
- Balance kindness with accountability, ensuring that empathy doesn't turn into complacency.

These findings support a fundamental truth: Too much comfort can be a trap. Employees who feel "safe" but lack challenge may stay in their roles without truly growing (Edmondson 2019). Leaders who focus only on creating a pleasant workplace may mistake passivity for satisfaction. Meanwhile, high performers who crave development and challenge will eventually leave for a company where they feel pushed and recognized (Buckingham and Goodall 2019).

On the other end of the spectrum, leaders who prioritize structure without empathy may create rigid, transactional work environments that lead to burnout and resentment (Kegan and Lahey 2016). Employees may produce results in the short term, but over time, stress, turnover, and disengagement increase because they don't feel valued as people (Goleman 1998).

Neither extreme—too much comfort or too much structure—produces high-performing teams. The best leaders find the balance between challenge and support, creating an environment where employees feel both safe and motivated.

Engaged Empathy Leadership Model is built on this balance. It recognizes that leadership isn't about making people feel good all the time—it's about helping them grow while ensuring they feel valued, heard, and fairly treated. The best workplaces are not those where employees are just happy but those where employees are engaged, driven, and inspired to do their best work.

Why Engaged Empathy Leadership Model Works

This is where Engaged Empathy Leadership Model (EELM) comes in.

A study published in the *Journal of Applied Psychology* found that leaders who demonstrate engaged empathy—active listening, clear communication, and structured fairness—improve employee retention and productivity by up to 47 percent (Smith et al. 2020).

Similarly, research from *MIT Sloan Management Review* found that companies with highly engaged leaders outperform competitors by 21 percent in profitability and 17 percent in productivity.

The message is clear: Leaders who engage with empathy—who balance kindness, fairness, and structure—create workplaces where employees don't just feel good but actually perform at their best.

This book isn't about guessing what works in leadership. It's about using what we know—what research, real-world case studies, and experience tell us—to build a leadership model that actually makes an impact.

CHAPTER 2

The Cost of Disengagement

If you talk to enough business *managers*, you start to hear the same complaints on repeat.

> "These young kids don't want to work."
> "They have no loyalty."
> "They're entitled and expect too much."

Most of the time, when managers say "these young kids," they don't actually know the difference between Gen Z and millennials. But regardless of the generation they're referring to, the problem isn't that employees don't want to work—it's that they don't want to work for leaders who aren't engaged.

And that's a management problem, not a generational one.

The Hidden Cost of Disengagement

Employee disengagement is one of the most expensive yet overlooked problems in business today. Companies focus on revenue, efficiency, and performance, but they fail to recognize how much money is bleeding out from employees who are just showing up, doing the bare minimum, and checking out mentally.

Numbers don't lie:

- Only 23 percent of employees worldwide are engaged at work (Gallup 2023).
- The other 77 percent? They're either not engaged (quiet quitting) or actively disengaged (hurting morale).

- Disengaged employees cost businesses between $450 billion and $550 billion per year in lost productivity (The Engagement Institute 2017).
- High turnover due to disengagement costs U.S. businesses an estimated $1 trillion annually (Gallup 2021).

Unlike past generations, they aren't afraid to leave a job that fails to meet their expectations. A report from LinkedIn found that Gen Z employees are twice as likely as millennials to leave a job within the first year if they feel unsupported or disengaged (LinkedIn 2022). Their decision to leave isn't impulsive—it's a response to environments where leadership is unclear, communication is inconsistent, and there's no clear path forward.

In my own research, I've spoken with managers who misinterpret Gen Z's desire for structure and transparency as "entitlement." But it's not entitlement—it's a sign of how workplace expectations have shifted. This generation grew up in an era of instant information, direct feedback, and digital transparency—they expect the same from their workplaces. When they don't get it, they don't just complain; they leave.

Here's the reality: Disengagement isn't always loud. It's not just the employees who are complaining, missing deadlines, or openly frustrated. In fact, the biggest financial drain comes from the ones who are still showing up, still collecting a paycheck, but doing just enough to avoid getting fired—quiet quitting if you will.

That's where companies lose.

How Disengagement Kills Profitability

When employees are disengaged, companies experience:

- Lower Productivity: Disengaged employees work at a fraction of their potential, completing tasks slower and with less care.
- Higher Turnover: Employees who feel disconnected from their work don't stick around, leading to constant hiring and training costs.
- Decreased Innovation: When employees don't feel heard or valued, they stop bringing ideas to the table.
- Poor Customer Experience: Disengaged employees lead to disengaged customers—service suffers when workers don't care.

One of the most telling signs of disengagement is the rise of "quiet quitting"—employees who stay in their jobs but mentally check out. They stop going above and beyond, stop participating in company culture, and stop seeing their work as meaningful.

The irony? Many of these employees started out engaged.

So, what changed?

Ask most disengaged employees why they stopped caring, and they won't say "because I'm lazy" or "because I don't want to work."

They'll say things like:

"I worked hard, but my effort wasn't recognized."

"Leadership keeps changing policies without telling us why."

"There's no path forward here—no matter what I do, it won't matter."

"I used to care, but I got burned out and no one seemed to notice."

That's the real problem. Disengagement *isn't* about laziness. It's about broken trust.

Employees become disengaged when they feel like their work doesn't matter, their leaders don't care, and their future at the company is uncertain.

Companies That Lost Talent Due to Poor Leadership Structures

Disengagement isn't just frustrating—it's expensive. Companies lose billions of dollars each year due to poor leadership, but behind every statistic is a real workplace where employees checked out, quit, or stayed but stopped caring.

The Hidden Cost of Chaos in Health Care: The Consequences of Leadership Without Structure

One of the most striking examples of disengagement came from a Gen Z health care worker I interviewed. She had only been on the job for a few months but was already contemplating leaving. Not because she disliked the work, not because of poor pay, and not even because of an overbearing boss—things that are often cited as reasons for quitting. Instead, her frustration came from something far more insidious: a complete lack of structure in her workplace:

> It's actually scary when I think about it. We are taking care of patients, and yet there is absolutely no sense of structure at all. Half the time, I'm not even sure who I am supposed to report to when I'm on my shift.

That statement says everything. This wasn't about minor inconveniences, scheduling headaches, or typical workplace frustrations. This was a patient-facing role in an industry where *mistakes cost lives*. Yet, instead of investing in structured leadership, the organization was hoping employees would just "figure it out." Instead of setting clear expectations, they created a workplace that left employees disoriented, frustrated, and anxious.

This is what happens when leadership assumes that employees will simply adjust over time rather than setting clear, structured expectations from the beginning. But Gen Z employees—more than any generation before them—are unwilling to tolerate that level of uncertainty. Unlike past generations who often expected a "sink or swim" experience in new jobs, Gen Z demands clear guidance. They don't just want to know what to do, they want to understand why it matters, how their role connects to the bigger picture, and where they can go from there.

For this health care worker, the lack of structure wasn't just making her job harder—it was making her question whether she could trust her own workplace. When leadership lacks structure, employees don't just disengage—they can feel unsafe.

The Hidden Cost of Disorganization

This frustration isn't unique to this one health care worker—it reflects a broader challenge with Gen Z in the workforce. Unlike previous generations, Gen Z employees expect both autonomy and structure—a balance many workplaces fail to provide. They want clear guidelines on roles and expectations, but they also want the flexibility to problem-solve and grow within those boundaries.

Unfortunately, many workplaces continue to operate with outdated assumptions about onboarding and leadership. The belief that employees should be able to "figure it out as they go" or that unclear expectations will somehow build resilience is deeply flawed. While previous generations, particularly baby boomers and Gen X, may have been willing to navigate ambiguity in the workplace, Gen Z views a lack of direction as a leadership failure.

In my research, I've heard similar stories across multiple industries. Gen Z workers describe feeling lost, uncertain, and even resentful when they enter jobs where leadership assumes they'll "pick things up over time." Many have had negative onboarding experiences where they were given little to no structured training and were left to shadow coworkers who were equally uncertain about leadership expectations.

A young marketing professional told me about her first job at a large corporate agency, where she was given a vague job description, minimal training, and inconsistent feedback.

> I kept asking for clarity on what was expected of me, but every answer was vague—"Oh, you'll get the hang of it" or "Just follow what others are doing." I had no idea what "good" looked like. I didn't know if I was doing well or about to be fired.

This lack of structure didn't just cause frustration—it made her feel disposable. When employees don't receive clear expectations, they don't feel like valued team members; they feel like replaceable parts in a machine.

The Leadership Gap: Why Traditional Approaches No Longer Work

One of the biggest generational shifts in workplace culture is the expectation of clarity.

Millennials—while also questioning workplace norms—were often expected to "pay their dues" by navigating unclear expectations and proving themselves through trial and error. Many accepted this reality as part of climbing the career ladder, assuming that ambiguity was just part of the process. Gen Z, however, doesn't see ambiguity as a necessary challenge—it sees it as poor leadership.

This shift isn't about entitlement; it reflects broader changes in communication, education, and leadership expectations. Gen Z has grown up in a world of instant access to information, where learning is structured, data driven, and interactive. They don't expect to have all the answers, but they do expect leadership to provide a clear framework for success.

When that framework is missing, they disengage—or they leave.

The reality is that employees don't just leave jobs; they leave leaders—not only because they had a bad experience, but because those leaders failed to provide what was necessary for them to succeed both professionally and personally in their roles. Leadership isn't just about setting strategy or managing teams—it's about creating an environment where employees can do their best work, grow in their careers, and feel valued for their contributions. When leaders fail to provide direction, support, and opportunity, even the most talented employees will eventually seek it elsewhere.

This is why Engaged Empathy Leadership Model (EELM) is critical. It ensures that leaders do not just engage employees emotionally but also provide the structured support they need to succeed. Without clear leadership, even the most driven employees will feel lost, undervalued, and ultimately uncommitted.

Companies that continue to rely on outdated leadership models—where employees are expected to figure things out on their own—will struggle with retention, engagement, and long-term success. But the organizations that recognize this shift and adapt will be the ones that thrive.

Those that don't will watch as their best talent walks out the door—not just in search of a better job but in search of better leadership.

A Culture of "Empty Suits" in Accounting

Disengagement isn't always caused by a lack of structure. In some industries, the real problem is a toxic culture that leadership refuses to acknowledge. That's exactly what I witnessed as an employee at a midsize accounting firm, where leadership spoke the language of employee well-being but failed to practice it.

One HR manager I spoke with put it bluntly: "This isn't easy to say, but the environment here is not ideal," he admitted.

> Honestly? It's a bunch of empty suits. We say all the right things about work–life balance, respect, and valuing employees, but it's just talk. If you strip away the corporate messaging, what you'll find underneath is a culture where people are stepping on each other to get ahead, management turns a blind eye, and leadership doesn't actually care about the well-being of its people.

One situation in particular stood out. A top-performing employee requested a temporary flexible schedule so she could care for a sick family member. On the surface, everyone—from HR to her colleagues—was supportive. But when the request reached management, the response was cold and final: "Not happening. Hours stay the same."

No conversation, no consideration—just a firm no.

"She was so hurt and in some ways shocked," the HR manager recalled. "She'd been a top performer, someone we really needed. But after that response, she left—and took one of her closest colleagues with her. Another great performer, gone. That was a really bad move."

The lesson? When employees realize the company only "cares" when it's convenient, they don't just disengage—they leave. And they don't leave alone.

A leadership team that practiced engaged empathy would have stopped this before it started. They would have created fair performance metrics, set clear promotion criteria, and addressed workplace toxicity instead of ignoring it. Instead, by failing to align their actions with their values, leadership drove their best employees straight to the competition.

WeWork: When Vision Lacks Leadership

While smaller organizations often struggle with internal politics and disengagement, even billion-dollar companies aren't immune to poor leadership. In fact, the larger the organization, the greater the risk that lofty messaging overshadows real leadership. Few examples illustrate this better than WeWork.

For years, Adam Neumann's leadership at WeWork revolved around an idealistic, high-energy startup culture. Employees were encouraged to work long hours, sacrifice work–life balance, and buy into the company's mission of "changing the world." The culture was electric, fueled by grand vision and relentless enthusiasm.

But behind the scenes, there was no real structure. Leadership ignored financial realities, causing the company to burn through cash at an unsustainable rate. Employees were expected to go "all in" on the culture, often at the expense of their personal well-being. Promotions and raises were inconsistent, leading to resentment as employees realized that opportunities were based more on favoritism than merit.

Eventually, the cracks in WeWork's foundation became too large to ignore. Employees who had once been deeply engaged and motivated realized that the inspirational messaging wasn't backed by real leadership. The company's implosion left thousands scrambling for jobs, disillusioned by the gap between vision and reality.

This is what happens when leaders rely on energy instead of engagement. You can make people feel good in the moment, but without fairness, structure, and clear decision making, they will eventually see through the facade. True leadership isn't about selling a dream—it's about creating a sustainable environment where employees can thrive.

The Lesson: Leadership Structure Matters

These examples, from small businesses to global corporations, prove one thing: disengagement is not an isolated issue, nor is it limited to one type of industry. The common denominator in all these cases is leadership structure—or the lack of it. Employees don't disengage because they're lazy, entitled, or unwilling to work hard. They disengage because leadership fails to create an environment where they feel valued, heard, and set up for success.

Disengagement isn't always about low pay, bad benefits, or employees "not wanting to work." More often than not, it's about poor leadership structures that make employees feel lost, undervalued, or unmotivated.

What do these case studies have in common?

- Lack of structure → Employees felt directionless and unsupported.
- Lack of fairness → Promotions and raises felt political or unclear.
- Lack of real engagement → Leaders acted like everything was fine instead of addressing real problems.

This is why Engaged Empathy Leadership Model matters. It's not about making people feel good temporarily; it's about creating a workplace where employees want to stay because they feel valued, respected, and supported by real leadership.

Key Takeaways from Part 1: Where Leadership Falls Short

The Misconception of Empathy in Leadership

- **Being nice isn't the same as being kind.** Leaders who focus on friendliness without accountability create surface-level connections but fail to earn lasting respect.
- **Real leadership requires action, not just intent.** Listening and understanding are valuable, but if they don't lead to meaningful decisions and support, they fall flat.
- **Performative empathy doesn't drive engagement.** Employees don't need leaders who simply make them feel good—they need leaders who create structure, fairness, and opportunities to succeed.

The Risks of Passive Empathy

- **Burnout happens when leaders try to please everyone.** Without boundaries, both leaders and employees become emotionally drained.
- **Favoritism creeps in when kindness isn't balanced with fairness.** The loudest and most charismatic employees often get ahead while true high performers are overlooked.
- **Emotional labor overload distracts from real work.** When employees feel like they have to manage everyone's emotions, workplace culture shifts from growth to avoidance.

The Leadership Engagement Gap
- **Most leaders think they're better than they are.** Studies show a massive disconnect between how leaders perceive themselves and how employees actually feel.
- **Employees don't leave companies—they leave bad leadership.** Research proves that poor management is the #1 driver of turnover.
- **Comfort doesn't equal engagement.** Just because employees aren't openly complaining doesn't mean they're happy, motivated, or doing their best work.

The Cost of Disengagement
- **Employee disengagement is a multibillion-dollar issue.** Companies lose hundreds of billions annually due to lost productivity, high turnover, and lack of innovation.
- **Quiet quitting is worse than loud quitting.** The biggest financial drain comes from employees who stay but mentally check out, doing just enough not to get fired.
- **Broken trust leads to disengagement.** Employees don't stop caring because they're lazy—they stop caring because they feel undervalued, unheard, or stuck.

Real-World Case Studies: The Price of Poor Leadership
- **Health Care Industry:** Lack of structure left employees confused and disengaged, proving that clarity is a core leadership responsibility.
- **Accounting Firm:** A toxic, political culture led top performers to quit, showing that fairness and transparency in decision making are nonnegotiable.
- **WeWork:** A feel-good culture without structure collapsed under its own weight, proving that leadership must balance energy with execution.

The Lesson: Leadership Needs Kindness, Fairness,
and Structure

- **Leadership isn't about choosing between results and relationships.** The best leaders balance engaged empathy with clear expectations.
- **People don't quit companies—they quit poor leadership.** If employees don't trust their leaders, they disengage or leave.
- **Engaged Empathy Leadership Model is the solution.** The best workplaces don't just feel good—they function effectively because they are built on kindness, fairness, and structure.

PART 2

The Solution—Engaged Empathy Leadership Model (EELM)

CHAPTER 3

What Is Engaged Empathy Leadership Model?

Conceptual Framework: The Shift from Feeling Empathy to Engaging with Empathy

If good intentions alone made great leaders, every office would feel like Disney World.

Most leaders don't set out to be bad at their jobs. They genuinely want to support their employees, foster a positive culture, and lead effectively. But good intentions without action are about as useful as a map you never unfold—nice to have, but it won't get you anywhere meaningful.

So why do so many still fail?

Because they stop at feeling empathy instead of engaging with it.

Empathy—understanding how someone feels—is a critical leadership skill. But understanding alone doesn't create results. Employees don't just need leaders who recognize their struggles; they need leaders who act on that recognition in ways that drive real change.

Too often, leaders believe that showing they care is enough. They listen, nod, and offer kind words, but their leadership style remains reactive instead of proactive. They assume that if they create a friendly and open work environment, employees will naturally feel supported and engaged.

But workplaces don't run on feelings alone. They run on systems, expectations, and accountability. Without those, even the most well-meaning leader will fail to build a culture where employees thrive.

This is where Engaged Empathy Leadership Model (EELM) comes in.

The research confirms this gap. In my qualitative study on Gen Z workplace engagement, employees repeatedly described situations where leadership was emotionally supportive but lacked the structure and clarity needed for them to succeed. Many young workers expressed frustration with leaders who offered words of encouragement but failed to provide clear direction, pathways for growth, or fair decision making. This misalignment between emotional support and actionable leadership led to disengagement, higher turnover, and a lack of trust in the organization.

Engaged Empathy Leadership bridges this gap by moving beyond emotional connection to real, structured action.

Research Insights: The Science Behind Engaged Leadership

There's a reason engaged leadership is more effective than passive empathy. Research on workplace behavior and leadership effectiveness consistently shows that employees perform best when they feel both psychologically safe and structurally supported. Without both elements, even the most well-intentioned leadership efforts fall flat.

A groundbreaking study by Google's Project Aristotle examined what made teams most successful. Surprisingly, the number one factor wasn't intelligence, experience, or technical skills—it was psychological safety. Employees need to feel like they can ask questions, take risks, and voice concerns without fear of punishment or embarrassment. However, psychological safety alone isn't enough to drive long-term engagement. Studies from MIT Sloan and Gallup have found that employees are most engaged when they also have clear goals, structured support, and consistent feedback. In other words, employees don't just want encouragement; they need leadership that actively builds systems and processes that help them succeed.

My own research on Gen Z leadership preferences reinforces these findings. Through qualitative case studies with both employees and employers, my dissertation revealed that young professionals consistently identified psychological safety as critical, yet many expressed frustrations that organizations focus heavily on inclusivity and emotional support without providing structured guidance study described their experience, saying:

My boss is really supportive and always says I can come to them with anything, but when I actually need help with direction or career growth, there's no real system in place. It's all just vague advice with no follow-through.

This statement highlights a common leadership gap today—managers are encouraged to be empathetic and approachable, yet without fairness and structure, employees feel adrift, uncertain about their progress and future.

My research found that fairness, structure, and kindness drive engagement. Gen Z employees highly value transparent decision making, structured growth opportunities, and leadership that is both supportive and accountable. However, without clear expectations, even the most empathetic leadership feels hollow.

- Clarity and structure matter more than flexibility—While many assume Gen Z prioritizes flexible work arrangements, my findings showed that 87 percent of employees preferred structured performance reviews and well-defined career paths over informal evaluations.
- Fairness impacts retention—Employees who felt where promotions, workload distribution, and performance evaluations were transparent—were 67 percent more likely to stay long-term compared to those who perceived favoritism or inconsistency.
- Empathy without action leads to disengagement—While 85 percent of participants agree it improves workplace culture, they also emphasized that without fairness and structured feedback, empathy feels performative. Leaders who listen but fail to act on concerns or apply policies inconsistently lose credibility.

The most effective leaders understand that kindness, fairness, and structure must work together for employees to feel safe to express themselves, supported by clear expectations and tangible opportunities for growth, is one where they don't just survive—they flourish.

For organizations, this means moving beyond superficial engagement strategies and focusing on tangible, transparent systems that allow employees to see a clear path forward. Leadership isn't just about making people feel good—it's about ensuring they feel valued, heard, and fairly treated while being challenged to grow.

By embedding fairness, structure, and engaged empathy into leadership practices, organizations can create workplaces where employees don't just feel supported—they thrive.

Practical Implications: Introducing the Three Pillars: Kindness, Fairness, and Structure

Engaged Empathy Leadership is built on three core pillars:

- Kindness is not about being nice—it's about creating genuine connections with employees and ensuring they feel seen, valued, and supported in meaningful ways.
- Fairness ensures that policies, promotions, and opportunities are transparent and equitable, eliminating favoritism and building trust.
- Structure provides clarity, direction, and expectations so that employees understand what is required of them and how they can grow within the organization.

Gen Z employees consistently emphasize the importance of these three elements. My research found that workplace dissatisfaction among younger employees often stems from a lack of clarity about expectations, inconsistent leadership decisions, and perceived favoritism in promotions.

One interview participant from a midsize firm described it this way:

I don't mind working hard, but what frustrates me is that no one really explains how to move up. It just feels like a guessing game, and when people get promoted, it's never clear why.

This is why engaged empathy must be more than just emotional support—it must be backed by clear structure and fairness.

Most leadership failures happen when one of these pillars is missing. Leaders who focus too much on kindness without fairness or structure create a workplace where some employees feel valued while others feel overlooked. Leaders who prioritize structure without kindness create a rigid, impersonal environment that stifles engagement. And leaders who emphasize fairness without clear structure or meaningful connection risk creating a workplace where employees understand the rules but don't feel inspired or supported.

Engaged Empathy Leadership requires all three. When Kindness, Fairness, and Structure work together, they create a culture where employees feel supported, motivated, and empowered to perform at their best.

The next chapters will break down each of these pillars in detail and show how leaders can apply them to create real, lasting change in their organizations.

CHAPTER 4

The Pillar of Kindness

Conceptual Framework

Leadership isn't just about scheduling check-ins; it's about engaging in meaningful, human-centered interactions that create trust, connection, and engagement. Employees don't want scripted conversations or obligatory check-ins that feel transactional. They want authentic engagement, where leaders meet them where they are, understand their individual preferences, and adapt to their comfort level.

A leader's ability to foster connection isn't measured by how many check-ins they schedule—it's measured by how those interactions make employees feel. When done well, these moments make employees feel valued, respected, and heard. When done poorly, they feel like another item on a manager's to-do list, a performative attempt at engagement rather than a sincere effort to connect.

Plenty of leaders figure they're already plenty kind—after all, they smile in the hallways, ask about your weekend, and keep their office doors wide open. But true kindness in leadership is more than just friendly chatter or being easy to like. It's about showing up in ways folks feel—in ways that stick. It's rolling up your sleeves when someone's struggling, standing beside them when things get tough, and proving with actions—not just words—that your people matter.

This means checking in when it matters most—not just during formal reviews or casual hallway chats but in moments of real need. It means recognizing when an employee is struggling without waiting for them to bring it up. It means offering support that is meaningful, not performative—whether that's adjusting workloads, providing resources, or simply being present when someone needs a conversation that goes beyond the surface level.

Employees don't just want a boss who nods in their direction; they want a leader who truly gets them—someone who looks past the job title and sees the person underneath.

Practical Implications: Casual Check-Ins: Beyond the Office, Beyond the Surface

A structured one-on-one meeting might check the box on engagement, but true leadership goes deeper. Employees open up and trust leaders when they feel seen as people, not just workers.

One employee I spoke with shared how her boss unintentionally built an incredible bond with her—by simply bringing her along to run an errand.

> It started as a quick trip to Target. We'd go grab some essentials after work, and slowly, these little outings turned into a routine. We found out we both let our kids pick a toy or snacks on each trip, and we started swapping stories about parenting, favorite decor styles, and even the best beauty products. It wasn't just small talk—it was connection. I looked forward to those moments because I felt like she actually saw me as a whole person, not just an employee.

This wasn't some grand leadership strategy. It was a small act of kindness that built trust, loyalty, and respect. Over time, these check-ins evolved into discussions about work wins, challenges, and personal growth. The employee felt valued, and the employer built a deeper, more engaged relationship with her team member.

For another leader, a blue-collar boss who ran a tough, hands-on crew, remembering personal details was a challenge. He admitted, "I care about my guys, but I've got a bad memory. I can't remember who has kids in Little League or who's got a wedding anniversary coming up."

I suggested he keep a small notebook to jot down key details about each employee—who was married, who had kids in sports, even favorite snacks and drinks. He started reviewing it before chatting with his team, and over time, he no longer needed the notes. His crew noticed the effort.

Eventually, he took it a step further. Before the annual Fourth of July celebration, he stocked up on each team member's favorite beer and snacks. He didn't make a big deal out of it, but his employees noticed. They saw that he cared—not just in words but in action.

This is what makes kindness different from niceness. Niceness is passive. Kindness is intentional.

Research Insights: Gen Z's Perspective on Leadership and Connection

Leadership today isn't just about authority—it's about authenticity. For Gen Z, personal connection matters more than traditional leadership formalities. Titles alone don't command respect; genuine engagement does.

In my research, Gen Z employees consistently emphasized that the leaders they trust and respect the most are the ones who take a real interest in them as people, not just as employees. They don't expect their bosses to be their best friends, but they do expect leadership to feel human, present, and engaged in a meaningful way.

Unlike past generations, Gen Z:

- Doesn't rely on hierarchy to define leadership. Just because someone holds a title doesn't mean they automatically earn respect. Leaders who engage with them in real, personal ways build stronger loyalty.
- Wants more than just "open door" policies. Many young employees feel leadership claims to be available but rarely initiates meaningful interactions. Passive check-ins aren't enough.
- Prefers leaders who meet them where they are. They value casual, comfortable interactions over forced, scripted conversations.

One Gen Z employee I interviewed described it this way:

I don't need my boss to be my best friend, but I want to feel like they actually know who I am. When leaders take the time to get to know what makes us tick—what we care about, what motivates us—it makes a difference. It makes me want to work harder for them.

Another described feeling disconnected from leadership because, while the company preached culture and community, no one actually engaged with employees beyond surface-level interactions:

> At my last job, leadership was all about "employee engagement" in theory, but I barely ever spoke to my boss. When I did, it was just standard HR check-ins. I don't need constant praise, but at least ask me something beyond, "How's everything going?"

This feedback highlights a generational shift in leadership expectations. Gen Z isn't asking for constant validation—they're asking for real connection. They want leaders who make an effort to know them, not just in performance reviews but in everyday interactions.

For organizations that want to retain and engage young talent, leadership must go beyond corporate messaging about culture and start practicing what they preach. Connection isn't built through HR policies or occasional team-building events—it's built through consistent, intentional, and personal engagement.

For Gen Z, leadership isn't just about authority—it's about accessibility. This generation was raised in a world where direct engagement with leaders, brands, and influencers happens in real time. Social media has broken down traditional barriers, making communication more fluid, informal, and personal. In their view, workplace leadership should feel no different.

Casual check-ins align with Gen Z's natural communication style—less rigid, more conversational, and built around genuine connection rather than strict professional boundaries. Unlike traditional top-down interactions, casual check-ins create space for authentic dialogue, where employees feel comfortable sharing thoughts, ideas, and concerns without waiting for a formal review.

By integrating meaningful, informal check-ins into leadership styles, organizations can:

- Build stronger trust and engagement with Gen Z employees.
- Improve retention by fostering a culture where employees feel seen and valued.
- Ensure feedback is fluid and reciprocal, rather than a one-way directive from leadership.

But here's the catch: Those check-ins have to be the real deal. If they come across as canned, forced, or straight from some "engagement play-book," Gen Z employees will sniff it out faster than your Grandma spots store-bought pie at Thanksgiving. They aren't after shallow small-talk—they want proof their leaders actually give a darn, not just that they're ticking boxes in some HR handbook.

Leaders who engage in authentic, consistent casual check-ins are the ones who earn loyalty, trust, and higher engagement from younger employees.

Kindness in leadership isn't just about showing care—it's about showing up.

For Gen Z and beyond, leadership must evolve from traditional, distant management to a model that prioritizes meaningful connection. Casual, intentional interactions aren't just "nice to have"—they are the foundation of a leadership approach that fosters trust, motivation, and long-term engagement.

Beyond Gen Z: Why Engaged Empathy Leadership Model (EELM) and the Pillar of Kindness Work for Everyone

While Gen Z has been at the forefront of demanding fairness, transparency, and meaningful leadership engagement, the need for kindness in leadership is universal. Employees of all ages—whether millennials, Gen X, or baby boomers—want to feel valued, respected, and supported at work. The difference is that past generations were often expected to tolerate poor leadership as a necessary part of the workplace.

Today, we know better.

Kindness in leadership isn't generational—it's foundational. People perform their best when they work in an environment where they are seen, heard, and treated with dignity. The Pillar of Kindness in Engaged Empathy Leadership Model (EELM) ensures that leadership isn't just about driving results, but about fostering human connection, motivation, and trust across all levels of an organization.

Different generations may have varying expectations of leadership, but the desire for respect, empathy, and connection is universal.

- Boomers and Gen X have spent decades in hierarchical work-places, often working under transactional leadership styles. Many of them appreciate the shift toward a leadership model that values collaboration and support over rigid authority.
- Millennials were the first generation to demand purpose-driven work environments and have long advocated for human-centered leadership. They respond well to leaders who treat them as partners in success rather than just subordinates.
- Gen Z, having grown up in an era of immediate access to leadership through digital platforms, expect approachability and direct engagement from their leaders.

The Pillar of Kindness in EELM bridges these generational differences, ensuring that leadership is inclusive, adaptable, and responsive to the needs of an evolving workforce.

Kindness Is Not a Weakness—It's a Strength

One of the biggest misconceptions about kindness in leadership is that it's all sunshine, handshakes, and ice cream—soft, passive, and about as effective as an umbrella in a hurricane. But here's the honest-to-goodness truth: Real kindness isn't weak, it's sturdy as an oak table, and when paired with fairness and structure, it sets the stage for teams to feel safe enough to take risks, dream bigger, and stay put when times get tough. After all, nobody ever built a barn just by smiling at the wood—you've got to grab your tools, roll up your sleeves, and show people you're willing to put in the work alongside them.

Studies consistently show that employees who feel valued and supported by leadership are far more likely to stay engaged and committed to their organizations. Research from Gallup found that employees who feel genuinely cared for by their leaders are 71 percent less likely to experience burnout and 55 percent less likely to be actively looking for a new job (Gallup 2021). Additionally, organizations that emphasize a culture of kindness and employee recognition experience a 40 percent reduction in voluntary turnover compared to those that do not (Gallup 2019).

Employees, regardless of age or experience, thrive under leaders who:

- Recognize and acknowledge contributions. No one, from entry-level employees to senior executives, wants to feel like their efforts go unnoticed.
- Show understanding and flexibility. Life happens—whether it's a personal crisis, family responsibility, or burnout. Kindness in leadership ensures that employees are treated as people, not just workers.
- Offer guidance, not just criticism. Employees don't just need feedback on what they're doing wrong—they need leaders who invest in their growth.
- When kindness is genuine and consistent, it reduces turnover, increases engagement, and strengthens trust. Employees are more likely to give their best work when they feel their leaders care about them as individuals.

Kindness as a Competitive Advantage

Kindness isn't just about building a pleasant workplace—it's about building one that works. Sure, kindness sounds sweet, like extra frosting on a cake you didn't ask for. But kindness is sweet like honey in a beehive. It's natural, necessary, and built through hard work, and without it, the whole system falls apart.

According to *Harvard Business Review*, organizations with highly engaged employees aren't just happier—they're 23 percent more profitable and have 41 percent lower absenteeism. Employees who feel genuinely valued and respected by their leaders are four times more likely to stay loyal, sticking around long after the latest workplace fad fades.

When leaders pair clear performance expectations with authentic human connection, they cultivate teams who lean in harder, think more boldly, and stick around longer. Teams who are:

- More engaged and motivated
- More innovative and willing to roll the dice on new ideas
- More likely to commit for the long haul

Kindness isn't a "nice-to-have" skill—it's the secret ingredient that transforms good leaders into unforgettable ones, the kind people tell stories about years down the road. It's the defining line between ordinary management and extraordinary leadership.

Leaders who practice Engaged Empathy Leadership Model aren't just guiding today's workforce—they're setting the stage for a new kind of leader, one who sees empathy not as optional, but as essential.

Practical Implications: EELM and Kindness Across Different Leadership Environments

Kindness in leadership is often misunderstood as simply being friendly or approachable, but in reality, kindness is about fostering genuine connection, trust, and psychological safety in the workplace. Employees who feel valued, understood, and respected are more likely to stay engaged, contribute at a high level, and develop long-term loyalty to their organization.

However, kindness does not manifest the same way in every leadership environment. A startup's informal, fast-paced culture requires a different approach than a structured corporate setting, a mission-driven nonprofit, or a remote workforce where employees may rarely, if ever, meet in person. Leaders who implement Engaged Empathy Leadership Model (EELM) must tailor kindness to the realities of their work environment, ensuring that it remains a leadership tool, not just a feel-good concept.

Startups: Kindness Without Burnout

Startups often pride themselves on being laid-back and people first, but this can sometimes translate into a lack of structure, leaving employees feeling unsupported and overworked. When kindness isn't paired with clear expectations and boundaries, it can lead to employees taking on too much, feeling obligated to "go above and beyond," and burning out quickly.

A common mistake startup leaders make is equating kindness with constant accessibility and overpromising flexibility. Employees are told they have a collaborative, open culture, but in reality, the lack of defined leadership roles and expectations causes stress, confusion, and resentment.

How EELM brings true kindness to startups:

- Set clear work–life boundaries. Leaders should model respect for personal time by avoiding excessive after-hours communication and ensuring employees take real breaks.
- Provide structured yet flexible support. Employees should feel empowered to take initiative without feeling abandoned in decision making. A kind leader in a startup doesn't just say, "Do what you think is best," but instead provides guidance: "Here's how we approach this—let's check in along the way."
- Recognize effort and progress, not just results. Since startups involve rapid pivots and frequent failures, kindness means acknowledging employees' resilience even when an initiative doesn't succeed.

Without structured kindness, startup employees can mistake exhaustion for commitment, sacrificing well-being in the name of company success. A kind leader in a startup ensures that the work culture is sustainable, not just exciting in the moment.

Large Corporations: Bringing Humanity to Bureaucracy

In large corporations, kindness is often reduced to corporate messaging, formal HR policies, and occasional "appreciation" e-mails. Employees may feel disconnected from leadership, viewing them as distant figures who only engage when something goes wrong.

A major challenge in corporate environments is that employees often feel like they are just another cog in the machine, where promotions, recognition, and workload distribution feel impersonal or driven by politics rather than people. Leaders may rely on formal employee recognition programs, but these often lack sincerity—an automated birthday e-mail or an "Employee of the Month" award doesn't replace real, personal appreciation.

How EELM fosters kindness in corporate environments:

- Make kindness personal, not just procedural. Instead of generic companywide recognition, leaders should directly acknowledge contributions—a handwritten note, a personal call, or a genuine compliment during a meeting can carry more weight than a formal award.

- Create spaces for genuine connection. Hosting nonmandatory leadership Q&As, informal meet-and-greet sessions, or reverse mentorship programs can help break down barriers between employees and leadership.
- Show up in times of challenge. Kindness in corporate settings isn't just about recognition—it's also about being present when employees are struggling. A leader who takes the time to check in on an employee after a tough project or a personal hardship builds long-term trust.

By humanizing leadership, corporate leaders practicing EELM create an environment where employees don't just feel like workers—they feel valued as individuals.

Nonprofits: Kindness That Strengthens Mission-Driven Teams

Nonprofits attract passionate, mission-driven employees, but that same passion can lead to high stress and emotional exhaustion. Employees in this sector often feel like their work is never done, which can create an unhealthy culture of self-sacrifice.

Many nonprofit leaders assume that since employees are driven by purpose, they don't need as much recognition or support—but this couldn't be further from the truth. When kindness is absent, nonprofit teams burn out at alarming rates, leading to high turnover, disengagement, and ultimately, a weakened ability to fulfill the mission.

How EELM ensures sustainable kindness in nonprofits:

- Acknowledge effort, not just impact. Since nonprofits work with limited resources, employees often take on multiple roles beyond their job description. Leaders must recognize daily contributions, not just major milestones.

- Encourage mental and emotional well-being. Leaders should actively monitor workload distribution, ensuring that dedicated employees aren't overburdened while others avoid extra responsibilities.
- Implement gratitude as a structured practice. This can be as simple as regular team appreciation meetings, personalized thank-you messages, or leadership shoutouts for behind-the-scenes contributions.

True kindness in nonprofits doesn't mean pushing people to work harder—it means ensuring they feel supported, recognized, and valued beyond their productivity.

Hybrid and Remote Work: Kindness in a Digital Space

Remote and hybrid work throws a curveball at kindness: How do you build a culture of connection when your team is just a collection of faces in little boxes on a screen?

Without intentional efforts to build relationships, remote employees can feel isolated, disengaged, and disconnected from leadership. In virtual settings, leaders may unintentionally show favoritism toward employees who are more vocal in meetings, while those who contribute quietly may be overlooked for recognition, promotions, and leadership roles.

One workplace I experienced firsthand successfully implemented EELM through structured yet meaningful virtual community-building initiatives. This included:

- Daily 5-minute stand-ups, where employees checked in on their progress and shared any challenges—not just about work but also about personal well-being.
- Weekly virtual happy hours, where team members played games, celebrated achievements, and got to know each other outside of work-related discussions.
- A digital Secret Santa program, where employees sent each other small gifts via mail, helping build personal connections despite the physical distance.

How EELM ensures fairness in hybrid and remote work:

- Implement structured check-ins that focus on both work and well-being. Leaders should reach out to employees beyond just performance updates to ensure they feel supported and connected.
- Use inclusive communication practices so that all employees have a voice, not just those who naturally speak up in meetings.
- Make celebrations and recognition intentional—leaders should acknowledge employee achievements publicly in virtual spaces to reinforce a sense of team unity.

Kindness in remote work isn't about grand gestures—it's about small, consistent actions that make employees feel seen and included.

Regardless of the work environment, kindness is only effective when it's intentional, structured, and embedded into leadership practices. A leader practicing EELM doesn't just hope for a positive culture—they design one, ensuring that employees feel seen, supported, and valued every day.

Whether it means setting boundaries in startups, humanizing corporate leadership, preventing burnout in nonprofits, or fostering connection in remote teams, kindness is not just a leadership trait—it's a strategy for long-term engagement and success.

By understanding how kindness looks different across industries, leaders can ensure that no matter where they work, employees feel a genuine sense of belonging and appreciation.

How to Structure Casual Check-Ins

For Employees Who Enjoy a More Casual Setting:

- Make it an outing, if they're open to it. Consider:
  - Grabbing coffee or lunch together.
  - Taking a short walk outside for a break.

- ○ Running an errand together, like a quick stop at Target or a bookstore.
  - ○ Playing a casual game of golf or attending a light social activity.
- Lead with vulnerability. Share something personal—a small challenge, a weekend anecdote, or even a friendly debate about the best coffee shop in town.

For Employees Who Prefer a More Traditional Setting:

- Make their environment comfortable. If an outing doesn't feel right, personalize their experience by having their favorite snack, drink, or coffee ready for the meeting.
- Remember small details. If they've previously mentioned a favorite show, movie, or sports team, reference it as an icebreaker to show that you listen and care.

Final Thoughts on Kindness: The Golden Rule: Personalized, Not Forced

- Ask, don't assume. Some employees love casual check-ins; others prefer a more structured setting. Let them decide.
- This isn't about hierarchy—it's about being human. Leaders should use these moments to show authenticity and build mutual respect.
- Consistency beats grand gestures—A one-time check-in won't build trust, but showing up regularly—whether in small ways or big ones—proves you mean it.

Casual check-ins aren't about productivity metrics or checking off engagement boxes. They are about fostering connection through intentional, everyday interactions. They show employees that their leaders see them—not just as professionals but as people.

One of the best examples I've seen of personalized kindness in leadership happened at a midsize company where I was consulting. A senior leader, Jason, had a reputation for being a strong, results-driven executive, but he struggled to connect with his team in a meaningful way. His check-ins felt routine, his efforts to engage employees came across as forced, and despite his good intentions, employees didn't feel a real sense of trust or connection.

During our meeting, I suggested that instead of defaulting to generic check-ins, Jason should take the time to learn what truly mattered to his team. Instead of just asking, "How's your week going?" he began tailoring his approach based on individual preferences.

For one team member, a die-hard baseball fan, Jason made it a habit to talk about their favorite team after a big game. Another employee had a child who has a recurring illness, and Jason checked in—not about work but about how the family was doing. He made a point to remember birthdays, favorite coffee orders, and even small wins employees mentioned in passing.

These weren't grand gestures. They were small, intentional moments of connection—and they made a tangible impact.

Employees who once felt like cogs in a machine started engaging more in meetings. Team morale improved without the need for forced team-building activities. Retention numbers ticked up.

The difference? Jason wasn't just performing kindness—he was practicing personalized kindness.

A simple conversation in the break room, remembering an employee's favorite coffee order, or checking in after a tough week might seem small, but these moments build trust. They send a clear message: You matter beyond the work you produce.

And when employees feel seen, they show up. They contribute ideas more freely, collaborate more effectively, and invest in the success of the organization as if it were their own. They work harder, stay longer, and trust their leadership.

Before Jason shifted his approach, employee satisfaction scores in his department were among the lowest in the company. Survey feedback indicated that employees felt unseen, undervalued, and disconnected from leadership. Many believed their contributions weren't recognized unless they actively self-promoted. Turnover was increasing, and morale was at an all-time low.

But after just 6 months of making these personalized adjustments, the department's engagement scores jumped by nearly 40 percent. Employees reported feeling more supported, more valued, and more motivated to contribute to the team's success. Voluntary turnover dropped, and Jason himself noticed a dramatic shift—meetings became more engaging, employees were more forthcoming with ideas, and productivity naturally increased without the need for forced engagement initiatives.

A simple conversation in the break room, remembering an employee's favorite coffee order, or checking in after a tough week might seem small, but these moments build trust. They send a clear message: You matter beyond the work you produce.

And when employees feel seen, they show up. They contribute ideas more freely, collaborate more effectively, and invest in the success of the organization as if it were their own. They work harder, stay longer, and trust their leadership.

That is the power of kindness in leadership—not as a one-time initiative or a feel-good gesture, but as a fundamental part of how an organization operates.

Addressing the Critics: Is Too Much Kindness Detrimental to Authority?

I get it. You might be thinking, *Sure, kindness sounds great—but won't too much of it undermine authority or blur necessary boundaries?* It's a fair question, and here's my straightforward response:

Kindness is not about softness. It's about strength. It's about having the courage to see people as human beings first and employees second. It doesn't weaken your authority—it enhances it. But, like anything, kindness must be balanced.

Here's where EELM gets it right: Kindness is never isolated. It's always paired with fairness and structure. That's the secret sauce. Without fairness, kindness might unintentionally slide into favoritism. Without structure, kindness might lead to unclear expectations or blurred boundaries. But with all three working together, kindness amplifies trust and respect, reinforcing—not eroding—your authority.

Let's also be crystal clear about something else: Kindness isn't a political stance, it's not a nationality thing, it's not a gender thing—it's a human quality. Kindness transcends demographics, cultures, and ideologies. The beauty of kindness in leadership is its universal power to foster connection, engagement, and loyalty, no matter who you are, where you come from, or what you believe.

Does kindness have limits? Absolutely. Can it be misapplied? Sure. No model is flawless. But the Engaged Empathy Leadership Model actively mitigates these risks by rooting kindness firmly in fairness and structure. That's why it works.

Kindness isn't about giving up authority; it's about wielding your authority wisely, respectfully, and effectively. And that's the kind of leader people genuinely want to follow.

CHAPTER 5

The Pillar of Fairness

Conceptual Framework

Fairness in leadership isn't about doling out equal slices of the pie—it's about making sure everyone knows the recipe. Employees don't just want a fair shot; they want to understand how decisions are made, what truly matters in the workplace, and where they stand. Whether seniority, merit, or a mix of both takes priority, the key is transparency. Clear expectations, honest communication, and real recognition aren't just nice to have—they're the foundation of trust, motivation, and a team that's willing to give their best.

Leaders often assume they are being fair because they apply the same policies to everyone. But fairness is more than just treating people equally—it's about ensuring that decisions feel rational, justifiable, and aligned with the organization's values. Employees don't necessarily need to agree with every decision, but they need to trust that those decisions are made with integrity. I like to say fairness isn't about giving everyone the same-sized shoes—it's about making sure everyone's fit right.

Many employees disengage not because they were denied a promotion, a raise, or an opportunity, but because they don't understand why. A lack of transparency creates resentment, leading employees to believe that leadership plays favorites, makes decisions arbitrarily, or ignores their contributions. When leaders communicate openly about what is valued in the workplace and how decisions are made, employees are more likely to stay engaged and feel a sense of ownership in their roles.

The best leaders create a culture of fairness by making expectations clear, ensuring employees know how they will be evaluated, and giving them a voice in the process.

Practical Implications: Creating A Culture of Fairness

Honest Communication About Growth and Advancement

- If seniority is valued, employees should be clearly informed so that they are not misled or left guessing about advancement opportunities.
- If merit is the focus, constructive guidelines should be in place to show how achievement is measured and rewarded.
- Employees should know exactly what is valued and prioritized, and these expectations should be outlined during onboarding and reinforced regularly.

When employees are unclear on what it takes to grow within an organization, they may assume the system is rigged, even when it isn't. Leaders should not shy away from explaining how decisions are made, even if it means telling employees things they may not want to hear.

Bonuses and Compensation That Reflect Fairness

- Implement achievement-based bonuses, where employees receive a standard bonus with additional amounts for specific accomplishments that align with company goals.
- Ensure transparency in how bonuses are calculated and awarded so that employees see a clear connection between performance and reward.

Many organizations claim to offer performance-based incentives but fail to explain how those incentives are determined. Employees should understand exactly what they need to do to earn additional compensation, and those who fall short should receive constructive feedback on how they can improve.

Constructive Guidelines for Advancement

- Employees applying for promotions or leadership roles should receive serious consideration, not just lip service.

- Establish a structured, transparent review process for advancement applications so that employees know their applications will be evaluated fairly and thoughtfully.
- Provide clear feedback on applications, ensuring employees understand why decisions were made and how they can improve for future opportunities.

Employees should never feel like they are submitting applications into a black hole. If they are turned down for a promotion, they deserve to know why. If leadership is committed to fairness, they will provide the guidance employees need to develop the skills required for future advancement.

Two-Way Feedback for Decision Making

- Leadership should be open about why decisions are made, particularly regarding promotions, compensation, and company policy changes.
- Employees should have a structured way to raise concerns about fairness without fear of retaliation.
- Consider quarterly "Fairness and Future Forums," where leadership discusses workplace policies, employee concerns, and potential adjustments in a transparent, solution-focused setting.

Employees feel more invested in their work when they believe their voices are heard. When leadership makes changes without employee input, even well-intentioned policies can feel unfair. Regular forums or structured feedback sessions allow leadership to explain decisions while also giving employees a platform to share their perspectives.

Eliminating Favoritism and Bias Through Employee Connection

- Use structured evaluation criteria for promotions, raises, and performance reviews to prevent favoritism.
- Encourage leadership training that focuses on reducing unconscious bias in decision making.

- Pull from the Kindness pillar—leaders who genuinely understand their employees and their strengths can make fairer, more informed decisions.

Fairness and favoritism cannot coexist. Many organizations unintentionally reward those who are most vocal or visible while overlooking employees who contribute behind the scenes. Leaders should make an effort to truly know their employees, understand their work, and evaluate performance based on merit rather than perception.

A leader who builds real connections with their employees is far less likely to make biased decisions. When leaders take the time to engage with employees beyond surface-level interactions, they can assess talent and potential based on real contributions rather than personal preference.

Research Insights: The Role of Fairness in Leadership

Fairness is often discussed as an abstract principle in leadership, but for Gen Z employees, it is the defining factor in their workplace experience. A workplace that lacks fairness—where promotions, recognition, and opportunities feel arbitrary—creates disengagement and resentment, no matter how empathetic a leader may seem.

In my own research, conducted across multiple industries—including technology, hospitality, education, and manufacturing—I found that fairness ranked as the single most important leadership quality for Gen Z employees. Leaders who prioritize transparency and structure in decision making foster greater trust, engagement, and retention among their teams.

One of the most revealing insights from my study was that fairness directly impacts retention. Employees who felt their workplace operated fairly—where promotions, workload distribution, and performance evaluations were transparent—were 67 percent more likely to stay long-term compared to those who perceived favoritism or inconsistency. Fairness, in this sense, is not just a moral principle—it is a strategic advantage for organizations looking to reduce turnover.

Fairness isn't just about treating everyone the same—it's about giving everyone a fair shot. That means making sure employees know exactly what it takes to get ahead, have a clear path forward, and trust that their hard work is measured by real standards, not office politics or favoritism. Because when fairness goes missing, even the most driven employees start to check out—after all, why keep climbing if the rungs keep moving?

My research also debunked a common misconception about Gen Z—that they prioritize flexibility over structure. While flexibility in work arrangements matters, my findings showed that 87 percent of employees preferred structured performance reviews and well-defined career paths over informal evaluations. This challenges the assumption that younger workers thrive best in unstructured environments. In reality, they want clarity, expectations, and measurable ways to track their growth.

Another key takeaway was that empathy alone is not enough. While 85 percent of participants agreed that empathetic leadership improves workplace culture, they also emphasized that without fairness and structured feedback, empathy feels hollow. Leaders who listen but fail to act on concerns or apply policies inconsistently lose credibility. Employees don't just want to feel heard—they want to see fairness reflected in the decisions that shape their work experience.

These findings underscore a critical truth about modern leadership: organizations that integrate transparent decision making, structured career growth, and engaged leadership models will attract and retain top talent. Fairness is no longer an optional leadership trait—it is a nonnegotiable for employees who expect clarity, accountability, and a workplace where effort and contribution determine success, not personality or proximity to leadership.

For leaders, this means taking a hard look at internal processes. How are promotions decided? Are expectations clearly communicated? Do employees trust that leadership is making decisions based on merit rather than familiarity? A company culture built on fairness, structure, and empathy doesn't just improve retention—it builds a workplace where employees can thrive.

Gen Z is often labeled as impatient in the workplace, but the reality is that they are driven by clarity and fairness. They do not see value in working hard for a company that keeps them in the dark. If they feel leadership is withholding information, playing favorites, or making inconsistent decisions, they disengage.

But when fairness is built into leadership from the start—when expectations are clear, pay structures are transparent, and feedback leads to action—Gen Z will work harder, stay engaged longer, and respect the organization's decision-making process, even if they don't always agree with every outcome.

Gen Z's Perspective on Fairness in Leadership

It's one thing for leaders to acknowledge that fairness matters—it's another to embed fairness into everyday leadership decisions in a way that employees can see and trust. In my research, Gen Z employees made it clear that fairness isn't about corporate mission statements or leadership slogans—it's about how decisions are made, communicated, and experienced in the workplace.

When asked what frustrated them most about leadership, Gen Z employees repeatedly pointed to:

- Ambiguous career progression. Many don't mind working hard—but they expect a clear path forward, not vague promises of future opportunities.
- Mixed signals from leadership. They would rather hear a direct and honest explanation about company changes than a watered-down version that lacks transparency.
- Inconsistent pay structures. They don't just want to know *how much* people make—they want to know *why* compensation differs among employees.

One Gen Z employee put it plainly: "I don't expect promotions to be handed to me, but I do expect to know how to earn one. If I feel like the process is random, I'll stop trying."

This generation grew up in the age of receipts—where leadership statements get fact-checked in real time and workplace fairness isn't just talked about, it's put under a microscope. The message is loud and clear: fairness isn't a slogan, it's a standard—and leaders who don't back up their words with action won't just lose trust, they'll lose their best people.

Beyond Gen Z: Why Engaged Empathy Leadership Model (EELM) and the Pillar of Fairness Work for Everyone

Fairness isn't just a leadership preference—it's a leadership expectation. While Gen Z has been vocal about demanding transparency, equity, and accountability in the workplace, employees across all generations thrive in environments where fairness is a core leadership principle. When people perceive bias, favoritism, or inconsistency in decision making, engagement plummets, turnover increases, and trust in leadership erodes.

Yet fairness is often misunderstood in leadership. Many organizations assume that fairness simply means treating everyone the same—but true fairness is about equity, not uniformity. Different employees have different strengths, career paths, and needs. Fairness isn't about rigid equality—it's about ensuring clear, consistent standards while recognizing that different individuals require different forms of support.

The Pillar of Fairness in Engaged Empathy Leadership Model (EELM) ensures that leadership decisions are not only transparent and structured but also aligned with employee expectations and organizational success.

Different generations have varying expectations about leadership, but fairness remains a constant across all career levels:

- Boomers and Gen X value merit-based advancement and expect their experience and tenure to be respected and rewarded fairly. Many have spent decades in rigid corporate structures and appreciate leadership that acknowledges their contributions while providing equal opportunities for continued growth.
- Millennials, who ushered in the era of purpose-driven work, expect fairness in leadership to go beyond individual career paths. They value inclusive workplaces where leadership decisions are transparent and ethical—not just for them but for the entire workforce.
- Gen Z, raised in an era of corporate accountability, expects leadership to demonstrate fairness in real, measurable ways—from pay transparency to unbiased promotion paths.

Fairness in leadership isn't a generational demand—it's a universal requirement for trust, motivation, and long-term engagement.

Practical Implications: The Business Case for Fair Leadership: Tangible Results

Fairness isn't just the "right thing to do"—it has direct business impacts. Research from McKinsey found that employees who believe their workplace operates fairly are five times more likely to be highly engaged than those who feel otherwise. Another study from the Society for Human Resource Management (SHRM) found that organizations with strong fairness policies experience 27 percent lower turnover rates compared to those with ambiguous or inconsistent leadership practices.

Employees, regardless of their generation, expect leaders who:

- Establish clear promotion and compensation structures. Employees who understand exactly how performance, tenure, and leadership potential factor into promotions are far more likely to trust the system.
- Communicate expectations consistently. Leaders who are transparent about goals, performance metrics, and decision-making criteria foster greater accountability and engagement.
- Hold everyone to the same standards. Fair leaders don't play favorites or move the goalposts based on personal biases—they ensure that the same rules apply to all employees.

When fairness is visible and measurable, employees work harder, trust leadership more, and stay with organizations longer.

Fairness isn't just a moral value—it's a business strategy. Organizations that prioritize fair and transparent leadership see measurable benefits:

Turnover reduction: Companies with structured promotion and pay policies experience 27 percent lower voluntary turnover (SHRM).

Higher engagement: Employees in fair workplaces are five times more likely to be highly engaged (McKinsey).

Stronger workplace trust: Fair leadership fosters a culture where employees feel safe to take risks, contribute ideas, and invest in the company's success.

Fairness is not about making everyone happy—it's about creating a leadership model where employees trust that success is earned, not given.

When employees believe their leaders act with integrity and fairness, they are more committed, more engaged, and more willing to contribute to a thriving workplace.

Organizations that embrace Engaged Empathy Leadership Model and the Pillar of Fairness don't just create better work environments—they build long-term trust, loyalty, and performance that set them apart in a competitive business landscape.

Practical Implications: EELM and Fairness Across Different Leadership Environments

Fairness in leadership is more than just treating everyone equally—it's about ensuring that all employees have access to opportunities, recognition, and advancement based on merit, not visibility or influence. When fairness is not intentionally structured into leadership practices, bias, favoritism, and exclusion become unspoken norms, whether leaders realize it or not.

However, fairness does not look the same across every workplace. A startup's fast-moving culture presents different challenges than a large corporation's bureaucracy, a nonprofit's resource constraints, or a remote team's visibility bias. Leaders practicing Engaged Empathy Leadership Model (EELM) must tailor fairness to each environment, ensuring that employees aren't left behind simply because of differences in personality, access, or circumstance.

Startups: Balancing Agility with Consistency

Startups are often praised for being agile, innovative, and adaptable, but this lack of structure can lead to unintentional favoritism. In many early-stage companies, leadership decisions happen quickly and informally—whether it's deciding who leads a new project, who gets equity, or who is promoted into leadership. Employees who speak up frequently, self-promote effectively, or build personal relationships with leadership may be rewarded more often, while equally talented employees who are less assertive but highly capable can be overlooked.

This creates an unfair system where employees feel like success is based on proximity to leadership rather than performance. A common scenario in startups is that high-profile roles or promotions go to those who make themselves highly visible, rather than those who produce the best results.

To prevent this, leaders practicing EELM in startups should:

- Create structured evaluation processes for promotions and project assignments to ensure decisions are based on measurable performance, not just leadership preference.
- Set clear criteria for advancement, rather than relying on vague promises of growth that disproportionately benefit those who are vocal or well-connected.
- Encourage introverted or quieter employees to take on leadership opportunities by proactively identifying talent and offering mentorship, instead of waiting for employees to advocate for themselves.

When fairness is built into the structure of a startup, employees feel secure in their contributions and trust that opportunities are available based on merit, not just who has the loudest voice.

Large Corporations: Preventing Bureaucratic Favoritism

In large corporate environments, fairness is often tied to hierarchy, tenure, and internal politics. Promotions may be dictated by who has the best internal advocates rather than who has the strongest performance. Employees often feel like they are competing in a game where the rules are unclear and leadership decisions lack transparency—leading to frustration, disengagement, and attrition.

A classic example of unfair corporate leadership is when an employee consistently delivers outstanding results but gets passed over for a promotion because they don't have a strong internal sponsor. Leadership may justify the decision as "not the right time" or "we need to see more," without providing any concrete reasoning.

EELM helps corporate leaders combat favoritism by:

- Making decision-making processes visible so that employees understand exactly how promotions, salary increases, and project selections happen.
- Applying structured performance evaluations consistently across all employees, ensuring that high performers don't get overlooked due to office politics.
- Actively seeking diverse perspectives in leadership discussions, rather than relying on the most visible employees to shape company direction.

When corporate leaders embrace fairness as a structured leadership practice, employees trust that hard work leads to opportunities—rather than having to navigate hidden rules or office politics.

Nonprofits: Ensuring Fair Workloads in Mission-Driven Environments

Nonprofits operate under different pressures than for-profit organizations, but fairness is still critical to their success. Employees and volunteers are often deeply committed to the mission, which can lead to uneven workloads and unclear career pathways.

One common fairness challenge in nonprofits: High-performing employees often take on disproportionate responsibilities simply because they care deeply about the mission. Meanwhile, others who contribute less may still receive the same level of recognition because leadership values loyalty over performance.

When workloads aren't fairly distributed, burnout increases, engagement decreases, and resentment builds. Employees start to feel like leadership expects them to sacrifice personal well-being for the sake of the mission—which is neither sustainable nor fair.

To promote fairness in nonprofit leadership, EELM encourages:

- Regular workload balance reviews to prevent top performers from being overburdened while others coast by.

- Defining clear pathways for career growth so employees know how they can advance, rather than staying in the same role for years without progression.
- Ensuring that passion does not replace compensation, by structuring equitable pay and benefits, even within budget constraints.

Fairness in nonprofits is not just about treating employees well—it's about ensuring that the mission can be sustained without exhausting the people who drive it.

Hybrid and Remote Work: Managing Visibility Bias and Big Voices

One of the biggest fairness challenges in remote and hybrid work settings is that certain "big voices" dominate discussions, while others get overlooked. Unlike in traditional office settings, where everyday visibility allows for natural recognition of contributions, virtual environments tend to amplify the loudest participants in meetings.

This creates an unfair system where employees who naturally speak up more—or have stronger relationships with leadership—get more recognition, while those who are equally valuable but quieter are ignored. Promotions, performance evaluations, and leadership opportunities may be unintentionally skewed toward those who are simply better at making themselves visible rather than those who deliver the best work.

For example, I witnessed a remote workplace where leadership regularly promoted employees based on meeting presence rather than measurable contributions. Those who consistently contributed in virtual discussions were rewarded, while others who excelled in execution but didn't self-promote were left behind. This led to frustration and turnover, as employees realized that effort alone wasn't enough—they had to "perform" to be seen.

To prevent this, EELM ensures fairness in virtual work by:

- Rotating meeting facilitators so that different voices are heard and the same individuals don't dominate discussions.
- Using structured participation methods like round-robin discussions or presubmitted insights, ensuring that quieter employees still have a voice.

- Implementing performance tracking based on work output, rather than meeting presence, to ensure that recognition isn't skewed toward the most outspoken individuals.

Without these intentional fairness measures, remote employees who contribute consistently but quietly may be overshadowed by those who command attention in virtual spaces.

Regardless of the workplace setting, fairness is not passive—it must be actively designed and maintained. It isn't enough for leaders to say they treat employees fairly; they must structure fairness into decision making, evaluation processes, and opportunities for growth.

Leaders who implement EELM ensure that fairness is transparent, consistent, and measurable—not dependent on personality, visibility, or proximity to leadership. When employees trust that hard work, talent, and results determine success—not favoritism or office politics—they are more engaged, more loyal, and more willing to invest their energy into the organization's success.

By recognizing how fairness operates in startups, corporate offices, nonprofits, and remote teams, organizations can ensure that every employee feels valued, heard, and given a fair shot at success.

Final Thoughts: Fairness as a Leadership Standard

Employees may not always agree with every decision, but when they understand how and why decisions are made, they are far more likely to accept them. When leaders communicate openly about promotions, policy changes, or strategic shifts, employees feel respected—even when the outcome isn't in their favor. The frustration doesn't come from not getting what they want—it comes from not knowing why.

Fairness in leadership isn't just about treating everyone the same—it's about creating transparency, setting clear expectations, and ensuring every employee feels valued for their work. It means:

- Eliminating ambiguity in performance reviews so that employees know exactly how their contributions are measured.

- Clearly defining pathways for career advancement, removing uncertainty about how to grow within the organization.
- Distributing opportunities based on merit rather than favoritism, seniority, or convenience.

A workplace built on fairness isn't one where everyone gets the same outcome—it's one where everyone gets the same clarity, opportunity, and respect. Employees should never feel like they are left guessing about their future within a company.

When fairness is embedded into leadership, it creates trust, engagement, and motivation. Employees stay not just for the paycheck but because they believe in the integrity of the organization and its leadership. And when employees trust their leaders, they give their best work—not because they must but because they want to.

Addressing the Critics: Can Fairness Ever Truly Be Objective?

Let's tackle the elephant in the room. You might wonder, *Is fairness even possible—or is it always subjective, always influenced by biases and personal feelings?* Here's my honest take: absolute, flawless objectivity—probably not. We're human. We have blind spots. But can we get pretty darn close? Absolutely, yes.

Fairness isn't some mystical ideal; it's a practical, achievable reality. It's about transparency, consistency, and clearly defined criteria. It's about openly communicating how decisions are made—whether it's about promotions, pay raises, or responsibilities. Fairness under the EELM framework doesn't pretend to erase biases completely; instead, it actively identifies, challenges, and mitigates them through structured processes and genuine accountability.

Here's why I believe this matters so much: Employees don't necessarily need perfection—they need trust. They need confidence that their leaders are doing everything humanly possible to make fair, consistent decisions. Fairness, when pursued intentionally and transparently, builds that trust.

So, can fairness ever truly be objective? Maybe not 100 percent. But under the Engaged Empathy Leadership Model, can we get pretty darn close? My answer is an emphatic, unapologetic yes.

CHAPTER 6

The Pillar of Structure

Conceptual Framework

Leadership isn't just about connection—it's about giving people a clear road map, not just a pep talk. Great relationships and good intentions are important, but without structure, they're like a car without a steering wheel—nice to sit in but not going anywhere. Structure creates fairness, accountability, and the kind of consistency that keeps employees engaged for the long haul.

People don't disengage because they dislike their work—they disengage because they're stuck in a fog. They don't know what's expected, how decisions get made, or whether they even have a future in the organization. And when the path forward is unclear, motivation takes a nosedive. Structure isn't about control—it's about clarity. It gives employees the guidance, support, and confidence they need to step up, lean in, and actually succeed.

Practical Implications: How to Build Structure in Leadership

A lack of structure in leadership often begins on day one of an employee's experience. Many organizations have onboarding processes that are vague, inconsistent, or overly procedural focused more on paperwork than providing a clear roadmap for success. Without defined expectations, employees can quickly feel lost, disengaged, or uncertain about their future.

A structured approach to leadership ensures clarity, consistency, and engagement from the very beginning—because nothing kills motivation faster than feeling like you're taking a test where the questions change after you've answered them.

Clear Communication Guidelines from Day One

When employees know what to expect from leadership, they feel more secure in their roles and more motivated to contribute. Establishing clear expectations early eliminates confusion and sets employees up for long-term success.

- Provide a structured onboarding roadmap that outlines roles, performance expectations, and company culture. Employees should leave their first few weeks with a strong understanding of what success looks like.
- Implement team charters that define roles, responsibilities, and collaboration guidelines. This helps employees understand where they fit within the organization and how they should engage with different departments.
- Introduce structured check-ins at key milestones (3 months, 3 months, and 1 year) to ensure employees are aligned with expectations and have a clear path forward.

By prioritizing communication from the start, organizations reduce turnover, increase engagement, and foster a workplace built on trust and transparency.

Two-Way Town Halls for Transparent Dialogue

Leaders often assume they are communicating effectively, but employees frequently feel left in the dark. Traditional top-down communication doesn't allow employees to ask real questions, challenge unclear policies, or gain insight into company decisions.

That's where Two-Way Town Halls come in.

- Held quarterly, these forums provide employees with a structured opportunity to engage directly with leadership.
- Employees are encouraged to ask questions, voice concerns, and provide feedback in an open yet respectful environment.
- Leadership offers real insight into company decisions, addressing concerns and ensuring employees understand key organizational developments.

- A moderator facilitates discussions, keeping them productive and ensuring that follow-up actions are documented and shared.

One employer who introduced these town halls admitted that at first, it felt uncomfortable:

I'll admit it was a bit awkward at first. But my employees asked great questions, and I was able to give them clarity and structured guidance about our vision. Awkward can be good.

That initial discomfort leads to growth. When leaders create a structured, open dialogue, employees feel valued, respected, and more connected to the company's mission.

Documented Policies That Everyone Can Access

Transparency builds trust, and trust drives engagement. Yet in many workplaces, policies and decision-making processes are unclear, inconsistent, or only referenced when issues arise. Employees should never have to wonder how decisions are made or where to find key company guidelines.

- Make all policies—including HR guidelines, promotion criteria, and performance review structures—easily accessible through an internal handbook or company portal.
- Use decision-making templates to ensure fairness and consistency in promotions, pay raises, and employee evaluations.

When policies are documented and accessible, employees feel empowered, informed, and confident in leadership decisions.

Meaningful and Continuous Training

A structured workplace invests in ongoing employee development, not just one-time compliance training. Employees should feel that leadership is committed to their growth and success.

- Go beyond compliance training—offer leadership development, resilience training, and skill-building workshops that support long-term career growth.
- Implement "Lead Like a Coach" training for managers, teaching them how to provide actionable, empathetic feedback that fosters development.

When training is consistent and meaningful, employees are more engaged, more committed, and more likely to stay.

Performance Feedback with a Purpose

The traditional annual review is outdated. Employees should always know where they stand—not just when review season comes around. Real-time feedback creates an agile, high-performing workforce.

- Shift from annual performance reviews to regular check-ins, providing employees with ongoing feedback and coaching.
- Implement a "feedback loop" approach, where employees receive real-time coaching instead of waiting for formal review cycles.

When employees receive structured, consistent feedback, they feel motivated, engaged, and supported in their development. They are less likely to feel blindsided by criticism and more likely to see a clear path for improvement and advancement.

Research Insights: Why Structure Matters

Structure does not mean rigidity—it means creating an environment where employees can thrive, innovate, and perform at their best. A well-structured workplace provides clarity, consistency, and accountability, ensuring that employees understand expectations, goals, and the pathways to success. Without structure, even the most talented teams can feel lost, uncertain about their roles, and disengaged from their work.

By implementing clear communication, transparent policies, meaningful training, and real-time feedback, leaders set employees up for success while fostering a stronger, more engaged workplace. Structure ensures that leaders aren't just making decisions reactively but are deliberate and strategic, guiding their teams with intention. It provides employees with the confidence to take initiative, knowing they have a reliable framework to support their growth.

The Pillar of Structure in Engaged Empathy Leadership Model (EELM) ensures that leadership is intentional, consistent, and results driven. When structure is thoughtfully applied, employees gain the clarity they need to grow, the stability to stay engaged, and the confidence to excel.

The Role of Structure in Leading Gen Z

Gen Z thrives in structured yet adaptable work environments. They are not looking for rigid, top-down leadership, but they do expect clear communication, defined expectations, and consistent feedback.

In my research, Gen Z employees frequently voiced frustrations with:

- Ambiguous job expectations. They want to know what success looks like and how they can achieve it.
- Inconsistent leadership communication. They prefer regular, transparent updates rather than sudden policy changes with little explanation.
- Lack of career development pathways. If they can't see a clear future within an organization, they will start looking elsewhere.

One Gen Z employee described their experience with unclear leadership, saying: "I'm fine with working hard, but I need to know what I'm working toward. If leadership keeps changing expectations or making decisions without explaining them, I lose motivation."

For leaders, this means that structure must be intentional—not restrictive but supportive.

A common misconception about Gen Z is that they reject structure. In reality, my research shows the opposite: Gen Z thrives when leadership provides clear expectations, defined career paths, and consistent communication. What they resist is uncertainty—unclear job roles, vague promises of advancement, and leadership that fails to communicate decision-making processes. Without a structured framework, they struggle to see a path forward, leading to frustration, disengagement, and turnover.

The Pillar of Structure in Engaged Empathy Leadership Model (EELM) ensures that leaders establish stability, transparency, and clear growth opportunities, allowing employees to navigate their careers with confidence. Structure isn't about micromanaging—it's about creating an intentional system where employees understand how success is measured, what career progression looks like, and how leadership decisions impact their roles. When leaders fail to provide this clarity, employees are left feeling adrift, leading to disengagement and high turnover.

Through my research across technology, hospitality, education, and manufacturing, I found that 87 percent of Gen Z employees prefer structured performance reviews and well-defined career progression over informal feedback systems. Employees in companies that provide clear role expectations and transparent promotion criteria report higher levels of motivation, stronger engagement, and longer tenure.

Conversely, when structure is absent, disengagement follows. One Gen Z employee described the impact of unclear leadership:

I'm happy to put in the effort, but I need to know where I'm headed. If leadership constantly shifts expectations or makes decisions without explanation, it feels pointless to invest myself fully.

A structured workplace isn't about rigid rules—it's about providing clarity, consistency, and direction. Employees, regardless of generation, perform at their best when expectations are fair, transparent, and clearly communicated. Leaders who implement structured feedback systems, clear career pathways, and transparent decision-making processes create workplaces where employees feel valued, empowered, and motivated to grow.

Strategies for Leading Gen Z (and Everyone Else!) with Structure

Define a Clear Career Roadmap

Gen Z is highly goal-oriented and wants a clear, step-by-step understanding of how they can grow within an organization. Ambiguous promises of "eventual" advancement don't resonate. Instead, they seek transparent, actionable pathways for professional development—whether through skill-building opportunities, leadership responsibilities, or structured promotions.

My research found that employees who had access to a clearly defined career progression plan were 67 percent more likely to stay with their company long-term than those who felt their future was uncertain. By laying out the roadmap for success, leaders create a workplace where Gen Z employees feel engaged, motivated, and committed to growth.

Move Beyond Annual Reviews—Provide Continuous Feedback

Traditional once-a-year performance reviews don't work for Gen Z. They expect frequent, constructive feedback that helps them course-correct and improve in real time. My research found that 82 percent of Gen Z employees prefer ongoing check-ins over annual reviews.

To keep Gen Z engaged, leaders should:

- Schedule regular one-on-one check-ins to discuss progress and development.
- Offer real-time coaching that focuses on growth, not just evaluation.
- Recognize accomplishments immediately rather than waiting for formal review cycles.

When employees receive consistent feedback, they feel supported, understand expectations, and can actively improve their performance—reducing misalignment and frustration.

Prioritize Transparency in Leadership Communication

Gen Z values honesty over corporate spin, and when they sense that leadership is withholding information, they disengage. Raised in an era of instant access to data and public accountability, they expect the same openness in their workplaces.

Whether it's a major leadership change, financial updates, or shifts in company strategy, keeping employees informed builds trust and prevents unnecessary speculation or anxiety.

In my research, 73 percent of Gen Z employees stated that a lack of transparency from leadership led to decreased motivation and trust. Leaders who proactively communicate company decisions—even difficult ones—foster stronger engagement and a culture of openness.

Providing structure doesn't mean stifling flexibility—it means creating a clear framework where employees can thrive. Gen Z doesn't reject structure; they reject inconsistency and unclear expectations.

When leaders define roles, career opportunities, and communication processes, they cultivate an environment of security, empowerment, and motivation.

The Pillar of Structure in EELM ensures that leadership is deliberate, strategic, and effective—not arbitrary or reactive. A well-structured organization doesn't just benefit Gen Z; it creates a stable foundation where employees across all generations can **succeed**. Because when the road is well-paved, the journey ahead is a whole lot smoother.

Beyond Gen Z: Why Engaged Empathy Leadership Model (EELM) and the Pillar of Structure Work for Everyone

Clarity creates confidence. Without structure, even the most talented employees struggle to perform at their best. While Gen Z has been vocal about the need for clear expectations, career pathways, and defined leadership processes, the truth is that every generation benefits from structured leadership. Employees, regardless of age or experience, thrive in workplaces where roles, goals, and opportunities are well defined.

The Pillar of Structure in Engaged Empathy Leadership Model (EELM) ensures that leaders provide the framework employees need to succeed—without micromanaging, stifling creativity, or creating unnecessary rigidity.

While Gen Z has been outspoken about the need for clear expectations and structured feedback, the desire for stability, direction, and fairness is universal.

- Baby boomers and Gen X value well-defined leadership processes and merit-based promotions that reward experience and expertise.

- Millennials appreciate structure when it provides clear career paths and leadership consistency, ensuring that opportunities are based on performance rather than office politics.
- Gen Z expects transparent, structured leadership models that allow them to see how their contributions fit into the broader company vision.

Structure Is Essential for Leadership Success

A lack of structure leads to confusion, disengagement, and turnover. Studies from Gallup show that 50 percent of employees don't fully understand what's expected of them at work, leading to lower engagement and productivity. Additionally, research from the *Harvard Business Review* found that companies with well-defined goals and leadership structures are 2.9 times more likely to retain top talent than those with unclear expectations.

Strong organizational structure fosters:

- Higher engagement. Employees who know exactly what is expected of them feel more confident in their roles.
- Better decision making. Leaders who provide clarity reduce workplace ambiguity, allowing employees to focus on execution rather than second-guessing their next steps.
- Greater career stability. A structured approach to leadership creates clear growth paths, reducing frustration and turnover caused by uncertainty about advancement opportunities.

Without structure, even the most well-intentioned leaders create unnecessary obstacles for their teams. Employees shouldn't have to guess what success looks like—they should have a roadmap to achieve it.

Structure Is Not Micromanagement—It's Alignment

One of the biggest misconceptions about structure in leadership is that it limits flexibility or innovation. Structure provides the foundation for creativity, productivity, and trust.

Employees across all generations respond positively to leadership that:

- Clearly defines roles and responsibilities. Employees perform best when they understand who is accountable for what and how their work contributes to the bigger picture.
- Establishes measurable goals. When expectations are specific and achievable, employees feel more motivated to reach them.
- Creates consistency in leadership. Leaders who follow a structured approach make decisions that feel fair and predictable, rather than arbitrary or reactive.

The presence of structure does not mean rigidity—it means alignment. Employees want to feel secure in their roles, confident in their contributions, and supported by leaders who communicate with clarity.

The Competitive Advantage of Structured Leadership

Organizations that implement clear, structured leadership practices see measurable improvements in retention, engagement, and performance.

Higher Retention: Employees in structured environments are 2.9 times more likely to stay long term (*Harvard Business Review*).

Increased Productivity: Teams with clear goals and accountability structures are 31 percent more productive (McKinsey).

Stronger Trust in Leadership: Employees who experience consistent leadership decisions are 3.4 times more likely to be engaged at work (Gallup).

Structure is not about controlling employees—it's about empowering them. When leaders provide clear expectations, defined goals, and consistent decision making, they create an environment where employees feel secure, motivated, and set up for long-term success.

Companies that embrace Engaged Empathy Leadership Model and the Pillar of Structure don't just create better workplaces—they create sustainable leadership models that ensure both employees and organizations thrive.

Practical Implications: EELM and Structure Across Different Leadership Environments

Structure is often misunderstood as rigidity, but in reality, structure provides clarity, stability, and a framework for success. Without it, employees are left guessing about expectations, career growth, and decision-making processes—which leads to disengagement, frustration, and ultimately, turnover.

Different leadership environments require different approaches to structure. A startup's need for flexibility is not the same as a corporate environment's need for process standardization. Leaders practicing Engaged Empathy Leadership Model (EELM) must recognize how structure influences engagement in startups, large corporations, nonprofits, and hybrid/remote work settings—and tailor it accordingly.

Startups: Creating Stability in a Fast-Paced Environment

Startups thrive on agility and adaptability, but this can quickly lead to chaos if employees don't have clear expectations. Many startup leaders believe that keeping things informal fosters creativity, but the reality is that a lack of structure often leads to burnout and confusion. Employees may struggle to understand who makes decisions, how performance is evaluated, and what their career trajectory looks like.

EELM helps startup leaders provide structure without losing flexibility by:

- Defining clear decision-making authority so employees know who to go to for guidance.
- Setting consistent check-ins and goalposts to ensure progress is measured without micromanagement.
- Establishing career progression pathways early to prevent high-potential employees from feeling stuck.

Startups that ignore structure risk losing their best employees to companies that offer more clarity and long-term stability. A well-structured startup doesn't stifle innovation—it creates a foundation that allows employees to focus on solving problems rather than navigating uncertainty.

Large Corporations: Preventing Bureaucracy from Stifling Agility

In large corporations, the challenge is often the opposite of startups. Structure exists—but it can be suffocating. Employees frequently get lost in bureaucratic red tape, rigid hierarchies, and slow decision-making processes. This leads to disengagement as employees feel like just another number in a massive system.

EELM ensures that structure serves employees rather than limiting them by:

- Streamlining internal decision making so that processes are clear but not burdensome.
- Implementing transparent performance review structures that focus on growth, not just compliance.
- Encouraging structured autonomy, where employees have clear guidelines but flexibility in execution.

The best corporate leaders balance structure with adaptability—ensuring that employees have clarity and predictability without the frustration of unnecessary red tape.

Nonprofits: Bringing Clarity to Mission-Driven Work

Nonprofits often struggle with limited resources, high emotional investment, and blurred job roles. Employees may be deeply committed to the mission, but without clear structure, they end up overworked, undervalued, and unclear on how to grow within the organization.

To bring structure to nonprofit leadership, EELM encourages:

- Defined roles and responsibilities to prevent burnout and workload imbalances.
- Sustainable workflow structures, ensuring that passionate employees aren't expected to "do it all" without support.
- Consistent professional development plans, so employees know how they can advance rather than plateauing in their roles.

Many nonprofits operate under the assumption that passion alone will keep employees engaged, but without structure, even the most dedicated employees will leave if they feel their efforts aren't leading to sustainable growth.

Hybrid and Remote Work: Structuring for Visibility, Accountability, and Connection

In hybrid and remote work environments, the biggest structural challenge is visibility—not just in terms of performance but also in communication, collaboration, and career progression. Without clear guidelines, remote employees can feel disconnected from leadership and uncertain about expectations.

One common issue in virtual workplaces is that certain employees—especially those who are naturally more vocal—tend to dominate discussions and get more visibility, while quieter contributors may be overlooked. When structure is weak, promotions, recognition, and opportunities often favor those who stand out in meetings rather than those who deliver consistent results.

EELM ensures that fairness and structure are built into remote environments by:

- Setting clear communication norms to ensure all employees have an equal voice, not just those who speak the loudest.
- Implementing structured feedback loops so that employees regularly receive guidance and performance insights rather than feeling "out of sight, out of mind."
- Using objective performance tracking methods that evaluate work quality and outcomes rather than presence in meetings.

Final Thoughts: Structure as the Foundation of Leadership

Even the most well-intentioned leadership efforts can crumble without structure. A leader may be empathetic, approachable, and supportive, but without clear expectations and consistent decision making, employees can feel lost, uncertain, and disengaged. Employees thrive when they understand what is expected of them, how success is measured, and how leadership decisions are made. Without this foundation, frustration builds, misunderstandings arise, and motivation declines.

Structure provides:

- Clarity about roles, goals, and expectations, ensuring that employees understand their responsibilities and how their work contributes to the bigger picture.
- Accountability in leadership decisions, preventing favoritism and ensuring that opportunities for growth and advancement are distributed fairly.
- Consistency that fosters trust and long-term engagement, allowing employees to feel secure in their roles and confident in the direction of the company.

A structured workplace is one where employees don't just feel supported—they feel empowered. They have the tools, guidance, and confidence to grow, take initiative, and contribute at their highest level.

But structure alone is not enough.

When structure is combined with kindness and fairness, it creates a leadership model that balances human connection with strong organizational foundations. The next chapter will explore how these three pillars—Kindness, Fairness, and Structure—work together to build workplaces where employees aren't just engaged, but deeply invested in their own success and the success of their organization.

Addressing the Critics: Does a Structured Environment Stifle Creativity?

This one hits close to home for me. You might wonder, *Does structure kill creativity?* With absolute certainty, I'd argue—no. In fact, I consider myself a creative person who deeply craves structure. Without structure, creativity can feel directionless, chaotic, even overwhelming. But give it the right boundaries, and watch creativity thrive.

Here's a real-world example from my classroom: Yes, it's structured like a lecture—students know exactly what to expect, when assignments are due, and how class discussions will run. But within that structure, I intentionally carve out space for creativity—open-ended questions, collaborative brainstorming activities, role-playing exercises, and strategic games where students can innovate, take risks, and experiment. It's precisely because they feel secure within the structured format that students feel confident enough to get creative—to truly think outside the box.

Structure doesn't stifle creativity—it unlocks it. It provides clarity, reduces anxiety, and creates a safety net that actually encourages creative risk-taking. That's what Engaged Empathy Leadership Model embraces—a structured yet dynamic environment where people know the boundaries well enough to confidently push against them, innovate, and ultimately, thrive.

Key Takeaways from Part 2: The Three Pillars of Engaged Empathy Leadership Model

Kindness: Meaningful Connection, Not Just Niceness

- **Kindness in leadership goes beyond being friendly.** It requires building genuine relationships where employees feel seen, valued, and understood.
- **Casual check-ins create real trust.** Meeting employees where they are—whether through an outing, a shared interest, or a small personal gesture—builds loyalty and engagement.
- **Personalized leadership fosters connection.** Leaders who remember details about their employees, like their favorite coffee or life milestones, demonstrate that they truly care.
- **Kindness should be intentional, not performative.** Employees can tell when leadership is simply "checking a box" versus when they genuinely invest in relationships.

Fairness: Transparency and Honest Leadership

- **Fairness isn't about treating everyone the same—it's about being honest and consistent.** Employees don't need to agree with every decision, but they need to understand how and why those decisions are made.

- **Clear promotion and compensation guidelines prevent resentment.** Employees should never feel like they're guessing how to advance. Leadership must provide structured, transparent criteria.
- **Feedback and advancement opportunities must be taken seriously.** Employees who apply for promotions or raises should receive real, constructive responses—not empty reassurances.
- **Favoritism erodes trust.** Leaders who build relationships with their employees are better equipped to make objective, fair decisions based on merit rather than personal bias.

Structure: Clarity, Communication, and Consistency

- **Leadership without structure leads to confusion.** Employees disengage when expectations are unclear, decisions are inconsistent, or growth pathways are hidden.
- **Two-way town halls create transparency and trust.** When employees can directly engage with leadership in structured forums, it eliminates uncertainty and fosters open dialogue.
- **A structured feedback system keeps employees engaged.** Shifting from annual reviews to ongoing performance discussions ensures employees always know where they stand.
- **Gen Z thrives in structured yet adaptable workplaces.** This generation expects clear expectations, transparent communication, and real-time feedback—not outdated, rigid leadership models.

The Bigger Picture: How Kindness, Fairness, and Structure Work Together

- **Kindness without fairness leads to favoritism.** Being friendly isn't enough—leaders must ensure opportunities and decisions are applied equitably.

- **Fairness without structure creates confusion.** Transparency means little if employees don't have a roadmap for success.
- **Structure without kindness feels cold and transactional.** Rules and policies must be balanced with empathy and real human connection.
- **Engaged Empathy Leadership Model is about action, not intention.** Leaders must move beyond passive listening and actively create an environment where employees feel valued, motivated, and empowered.

By mastering these three pillars, leaders don't just improve morale—they create workplaces where employees want to stay, grow, and contribute to long-term success.

PART 3

Application—How to Implement EELM in Your Organization

Coaching Leaders to Balance Empathy and Action: Implementing the Pillar of Kindness

Research Insights: Kindness as a Leadership Strategy

Kindness in leadership is not about being weak—it's about being intentional in how you lead. Leaders who integrate kindness with fairness and structure create workplaces where employees are not only engaged but also motivated to grow, perform, and contribute at their highest level.

To train leaders in balancing kindness with professionalism, organizations should:

- Emphasize that kindness is about respect and engagement, not avoiding difficult conversations. Many leaders equate kindness with being "nice," which can lead to avoidance of difficult conversations. My research found that employees, especially Gen Z, value leaders who provide direct, transparent feedback rather than sugarcoating issues. One participant stated, *"I don't need my boss to be my friend, but I do need them to tell me the truth."* Leadership training should focus on how to deliver constructive criticism in a way that reinforces support, rather than making employees feel singled out or discouraged.
- Provide coaching on how to deliver feedback in a way that is constructive rather than discouraging. Leaders who are either too critical or too passive create disengagement. Employees in my study described workplaces where managers would either avoid giving necessary feedback or deliver it in a way that felt

demoralizing. Psychological safety plays a key role here. Training should teach leaders to set clear expectations, frame feedback as an opportunity for growth, and ensure employees feel supported rather than attacked. Encouraging consistent feedback loops prevents performance discussions from feeling sudden or overwhelming.

- Set clear boundaries between personal and professional relationships. Employees disengage when they feel favoritism is at play. My research found that in some workplaces, managers form stronger bonds with certain employees, which leads to imbalances in promotions, raises, and opportunities. One HR leader I interviewed noted that their company struggled because "if you had the right personal relationship with leadership, your career moved faster. If you didn't, you were left in the dark." Leadership training should focus on how to build genuine relationships with employees without compromising fairness.

- Encourage a leadership style that is approachable but firm. Kindness does not mean letting things slide or being overly accommodating. Employees respond best to leaders who set clear expectations while making them feel valued. My research found that Gen Z employees, in particular, are more engaged when they know where they stand at all times. One interviewee stated, "I respect my boss because I always know what they expect of me. They're a little tough but fair." Leaders should be trained to maintain an approachable yet structured leadership style that reinforces both accountability and trust.

Kindness does not mean letting things slide or avoiding confrontation. Leaders who are both kind and professional create an environment where employees feel safe to communicate openly while still being held accountable for their work.

Using Employee Preferences to Tailor Engagement

A one-size-fits-all approach to leadership rarely works, and kindness is no exception. Some employees thrive in informal, social interactions, while others prefer structured engagement with clear expectations. Effective leaders recognize and respect these differences, tailoring their approach to ensure that every employee feels valued in a way that suits their comfort level.

Kindness in leadership isn't about treating everyone the same—it's about understanding what makes each employee feel supported, heard, and motivated.

To accommodate different engagement styles, organizations should focus on flexibility, personalization, and intentional leadership interactions.

Some employees feel comfortable sharing thoughts casually over coffee or in a quick hallway conversation, while others prefer structured meetings where they have time to prepare their thoughts.

Leadership should provide varied engagement opportunities that allow employees to connect in ways that feel natural to them. When employees feel in control of how they engage with leadership, they are more likely to share honest feedback and build trust.

Not all employees express themselves the same way. Some may be more reserved in group settings but open up in one-on-one discussions. Others may thrive in spontaneous conversations but feel uncomfortable in formal check-ins.

Leaders must be trained to notice these differences and adapt accordingly.

Incorporating simple tools like periodic engagement preference surveys can help gauge where employees feel most comfortable. Managers should also be encouraged to experiment with different forms of engagement—sometimes, a conversation that starts in an office might naturally transition into a walk around the parking lot for fresh air. Spontaneity is OK, as long as employees feel comfortable.

The key is intentionality—leaders should never assume they know what employees prefer without asking.

Creating a Mix of Engagement Opportunities

A truly engaged workplace doesn't rely on just one form of communication. Leadership should facilitate a variety of engagement methods that allow employees to interact in ways that feel authentic.

Some effective approaches include:

- Informal team outings or coffee chats to encourage casual, low-pressure interactions.
- Structured one-on-one meetings for employees who feel more comfortable with direct, focused conversations.
- Anonymous feedback channels for those who prefer to share their thoughts in writing rather than in person.
- Virtual check-ins for remote employees who may not have the same organic opportunities for engagement as in-office workers.

By giving employees choices in how they connect with leadership, organizations ensure that kindness isn't just a vague leadership principle—it's a personalized, thoughtful experience that resonates with every employee.

Encouraging Employees to Share Their Preferred Communication Styles Early

Engagement preferences shouldn't be an afterthought—they should be incorporated from the moment an employee joins the organization. During onboarding, managers should ask employees how they prefer to communicate and receive feedback.

Some key questions might include:

- Do you prefer direct feedback in real time, or written feedback you can process first?
- Are you more comfortable sharing ideas in group meetings or in one-on-one discussions?
- Would you rather have regular check-ins or only touch base when necessary?

Knowing these preferences early allows managers to build trust from the start. And just as importantly, employees should feel free to adjust their preferences over time.

By allowing flexibility in leadership engagement, organizations ensure that kindness is not just an expectation but an experience that makes every employee feel valued and supported.

Kindness in leadership is not about grand gestures or occasional efforts—it's about building an organizational culture where respect, connection, and engagement are embedded into daily interactions. Leaders who implement structured, thoughtful approaches to kindness create workplaces where employees feel valued at every level. When done well, kindness becomes more than a leadership trait; it becomes the foundation of a thriving company culture.

But kindness requires effort. It's not always easy because it's a choice. You can fake being nice, but you can't fake being kind. Nice is about surface-level politeness—kindness is about intentional action. It takes effort to be a leader who remembers the details, follows through on support, and treats employees as individuals.

My research confirms that Gen Z places high value on empathetic leadership, but not in a superficial way. They don't want leaders who just smile and say the right things—they want leaders who show genuine care through action. In a study of 250 Gen Z employees across multiple industries, 85 percent said that psychological safety, built through empathy and support, is a nonnegotiable for workplace satisfaction. However, they also made it clear that empathy alone is not enough. Without fairness and structure, kindness feels empty.

One participant in my research explained, "I appreciate when my boss checks in, but it has to feel real. If they ask how I'm doing but don't actually listen, or nothing changes, then it's just performative. I don't need small talk—I need leadership that actually cares."

This is why kindness in leadership requires more than just words—it requires consistency, intentionality, and follow-through. Gen Z employees, more than previous generations, actively evaluate their leaders based on how well their actions align with their words. When leaders fail to provide real engagement, Gen Z employees disengage or leave.

All of us—regardless of generation—could benefit from practicing kindness in a more deliberate way.

This reminds me of someone I admire: Fred Rogers. Many people think of him as soft-spoken and gentle, but his approach to kindness was radical. He didn't see kindness as passive—it was a deliberate, daily commitment to making others feel seen, heard, and valued.

One of my favorite quotes from him is: "There are three ways to ultimate success: The first way is to be kind. The second way is to be kind. The third way is to be kind."

What made Fred Rogers' kindness so powerful wasn't that he was always pleasant—it was that he was intentional. He listened deeply, responded thoughtfully, and treated every person with dignity. That's what real kindness in leadership looks like. It's not about empty pleasantries or performative gestures—it's about showing up every day with purpose, making an effort, and leading with empathy in action.

Building Genuine Employee Connections in a Scalable Way

Kindness in leadership isn't about random good deeds or the occasional pep talk—it's about building a workplace where trust, respect, and belonging aren't just nice ideas, but the way things are done. Too often, leaders worry that real connection doesn't scale, that as their company grows, there's just no time for one-on-one engagement. But here's the truth: organizations that weave kindness into their leadership see stronger retention, better performance, and a workforce that actually cares about the work they do.

When kindness becomes part of the company's DNA, it stops being about individual moments and starts shaping the entire culture. Leaders don't need to know every employee's life story—but they do need to create an environment where people feel valued, respected, and like they matter. Because when people know they're more than just a cog in the machine, they don't just show up—they show up ready to give their best.

Practical Implications: Step-by-Step—How Leaders Can Apply Kindness in Leadership

Structuring Casual Check-Ins at Scale

The most effective leaders create systems that allow personal connections to happen naturally, rather than treating kindness as an occasional effort. Casual check-ins are a proven way to build trust and engagement, but without structure, they often get deprioritized in the fast pace of day-to-day operations.

To ensure casual check-ins become a regular part of leadership, organizations should:

- Schedule brief, informal one-on-one conversations between managers and employees on a recurring basis. These should be distinct from performance reviews and focused on open dialogue.
- Encourage leaders to check in with employees in ways that feel natural. Some teams may prefer scheduled coffee chats, while others may thrive with more impromptu conversations.
- Rotate check-ins so that employees at all levels of an organization feel seen, not just those in high-profile or vocal roles.
- Use teamwide check-in practices, such as daily stand-ups or weekly roundtables, to reinforce connection without requiring constant one-on-one meetings.

Leaders should also ensure that casual check-ins don't feel forced or transactional. Employees can sense when an interaction is being done out of obligation rather than genuine interest. The goal is to create a culture where regular, meaningful engagement is the norm.

Case Study Example: Training Leaders to Balance Kindness with Professionalism

One of the biggest challenges in implementing kindness at scale is ensuring that it is not mistaken for weakness or a lack of accountability. Many leaders, especially in traditional, high-pressure, or blue-collar industries, worry that being too kind will make them seem less authoritative, less respected, or less in control. They've been conditioned to believe that leadership is about toughness, detachment, and unwavering authority—not connection.

But kindness and strength are not opposites. A leader can be firm yet fair, direct yet empathetic, approachable yet respected.

I once worked with a blue-collar leader who wrestled with this exact problem. He pulled me aside after a session and said, "Look, I get what you're saying, but I don't want to come off as soft. If I start being too nice, they'll walk all over me."

His whole leadership style had been built around toughness, straight talk, and keeping a professional distance. He genuinely wanted to connect with his team—but not at the cost of his authority.

I leaned in and asked, "Who's the kindest person you've ever known? Not the nicest—the kindest."

He squinted, thinking it over. "Probably my uncle," he finally said.

"What made him so kind?" I pressed.

He hesitated, then shrugged. "I don't know…he was just someone people wanted to talk to. He always remembered things about you that others didn't. And he actually helped."

"Like what?" I asked.

He sighed, then let out a small laugh. "So I was terrible at English in school—lit especially. And somehow, my uncle always remembered that. He'd check in, ask if I needed help, even joke about it. It was his way of looking out for me."

I nodded. "Did that make you feel awkward?"

"No, it was nice," he admitted.

"Did you ever think he was weak?"

He scoffed, shaking his head. "Hell no. He was tough as nails—just happened to love to read."

I smiled. "That's exactly my point."

His uncle didn't lose respect by being kind. He built trust by paying attention, showing he cared, and following through. That's leadership—not softness, not weakness. Just someone strong enough to care.

Kindness as a Leadership Strategy, Not a Soft Skill

This is where many leaders get kindness wrong. It's not about being soft or sidestepping tough conversations. And it's certainly not about lowering the bar. Kindness in leadership is about creating the kind of environment where people feel respected, supported, and driven to bring their best—not because they're afraid to fail, but because they know someone has their back.

A leader who takes the time to understand their team—who sees both the effort and the obstacles, who shows up during the hard days, and who treats people like humans instead of headcount—doesn't lose credibility. They gain it.

Kindness doesn't dilute accountability—it sharpens it. Because when people feel seen and trusted, they take more ownership, not less.

The best leaders aren't the loudest in the room or the quickest to lay down the law. They're the ones who know how to set the bar high *and* help people reach it. The ones who lead with clarity, consistency, and a whole lot of humanity.

And the leaders who get that? They're not just giving directions—they're being followed for a reason.

Implementing kindness in leadership does not mean lowering expectations or avoiding difficult conversations—it means fostering an environment of mutual respect, clear communication, and accountability. Leaders who balance kindness with professionalism set a tone where employees feel valued, engaged, and motivated to perform at their best.

My research found that Gen Z employees prefer direct feedback over vague reassurance. They don't want to be shielded from constructive criticism—they want clarity, honesty, and a clear path for improvement.

Leaders should be trained to give clear, constructive feedback that fosters growth without feeling punitive. Kindness does not mean sugarcoating the truth—it means delivering it in a way that is fair, productive, and solutions focused.

Teaching Leaders to Deliver Feedback That Is Constructive, Not Discouraging

Many employee's express frustration with leaders who swing too far in either direction—some come down like a hammer on every mistake, while others let things slide until the wheels fall off. When leaders are overly critical, they create a culture of fear where folks keep their heads down and play it safe. But when they're too hands-off, underperformance festers—and the people who *are* pulling their weight start to wonder why they bother.

That's why leadership training should focus on building psychological safety—the kind of team culture where people know feedback is meant to help, not humiliate. It's the difference between a coach on the sidelines and a referee looking to throw a flag.

Leaders also need to treat feedback like watering a plant—you don't dump a gallon on it once a year and hope it thrives. You check in regularly, a little at a time, so nothing catches folks off guard. When feedback becomes a natural part of the day-to-day, it loses its sting and becomes what it should've been all along: a tool for growth, not a weapon.

Leaders should learn how to build strong relationships with their teams without allowing those connections to cloud their judgment. Training should emphasize the importance of fair and structured decision making, ensuring that all employees feel valued and respected based on their contributions rather than their social capital.

Kindness does not mean letting things slide. Employees respect leaders who set clear expectations while remaining supportive. Leaders should be trained to hold employees accountable while still making them feel valued and respected.

When employees understand that leadership is both firm and fair, they are more likely to take ownership of their responsibilities while feeling confident that their leaders have their best interests at heart. Leaders who master this balance create a work environment where employees trust leadership, feel safe to communicate openly, and remain engaged in their work.

Practical Implications: HR's Role in Embedding Kindness in Workplace Culture

Human resources (HR) plays a critical role in ensuring that kindness isn't just an individual leadership trait, but an organizational standard. While some managers may naturally lead with empathy and connection, kindness-driven leadership must be institutionalized through policies, training, and companywide initiatives to ensure consistency across all teams.

HR should focus on two key areas to ensure kindness is not just encouraged but actively embedded into workplace culture:

1. Encouraging managers to take employee well-being seriously— making kindness a leadership expectation, not just a personality trait.

2. Designing workplace policies that support human connection—ensuring that organizational systems reinforce rather than undermine a culture of support and engagement.

One of the most effective ways to ensure accountability in embedding kindness into workplace culture is to establish key performance indicators (KPIs) that track how well kindness-driven initiatives are working.

KPIs for Measuring Kindness in the Workplace

To create real, measurable change, HR must implement clear KPIs that hold leadership accountable for fostering a culture of kindness. These metrics ensure that kindness is not just a value but an operational priority.

Employee Engagement and Satisfaction Scores

Kindness in leadership should directly influence employee engagement and workplace satisfaction. Surveys should include questions specific to leadership kindness and connection to track whether employees feel valued and supported.

KPI Target: Eighty percent or more of employees report that their manager demonstrates care and support in their professional development.

Survey Question Example: "I feel my manager genuinely cares about my well-being and professional growth." (Scale of 1–5)

If scores are low, HR should conduct follow-up interviews and leadership training refreshers to improve manager–employee interactions.

Retention Rates (Especially Among New Hires and High Performers)

Employees don't leave companies—they leave toxic or indifferent leadership. A lack of engagement from leadership is one of the biggest drivers of high turnover, especially among new hires and high-performing employees.

KPI Target: Reduce voluntary turnover by 15 percent among employees within their first 2 years.

HR should also track exit interview data for mentions of:

- Lack of leadership support
- Feelings of favoritism or exclusion
- Poor leadership engagement

Retention rates provide direct insight into whether kindness is truly part of leadership or if employees feel disconnected from their managers.

Manager Check-In Frequency and Effectiveness

If kindness is truly an embedded leadership standard, structured, meaningful check-ins should be a nonnegotiable part of how managers engage with their teams.

KPI Target: Hundred percent of managers conduct at least one structured employee check-in per month that focuses on growth, well-being, and engagement.

HR should implement automated tracking through HR software or require managers to log informal and formal check-ins to ensure these conversations are happening. If engagement is low, HR can reinforce the expectation through leadership coaching and accountability measures.

Peer Recognition and Employee-to-Employee Engagement

Kindness in leadership should not just flow from the top down—it should be ingrained in company culture at every level. A workplace where peer-to-peer recognition thrives is one where kindness is deeply embedded.

KPI Target: Increase peer recognition submissions by 20 percent in a year through formal platforms like Kudos Slack.

HR should track participation rates in peer recognition programs and analyze feedback on team dynamics to ensure kindness is an active part of daily interactions.

Manager Training Completion Rates

Kindness-driven leadership is not an innate skill—it must be taught and reinforced. If organizations want kindness to be a real leadership competency, they must train managers on how to lead with empathy, fairness, and structure.

KPI Target: Hundred percent of new managers complete a "Leading with Empathy" training program within 6 months of promotion.

HR should track completion rates and follow up with post-training surveys to assess how confident leaders feel in applying kindness-based leadership skills in real situations.

Survey Example: "How confident do you feel in applying kindness-based leadership strategies in your team?"

Low confidence scores indicate a need for ongoing support and refresher training.

Employee Well-Being Program Participation

A company that prioritizes kindness in leadership must also invest in well-being initiatives. However, if employees aren't utilizing these programs, something is missing.

KPI Target: Increase participation in employee wellness programs (mental health resources, mentoring, or well-being check-ins) by 25 percent within a year.

HR should track:

- Utilization rates of available well-being services
- Manager participation in promoting and normalizing well-being programs
- Barriers to access (Are employees aware of these programs? Do they feel comfortable using them?)

When kindness in leadership aligns with tangible well-being efforts, employees are more likely to trust leadership and feel supported in their workplace.

Fairness and Inclusivity in Leadership Decisions

Kindness means more than just being "nice"—it means ensuring fairness in how employees are treated, recognized, and promoted. If employees don't believe leadership decisions are fair, kindness efforts will feel hollow.

KPI Target: Eighty-five percent of employees report feeling that promotions and opportunities are based on merit and not favoritism.

HR should measure fairness through:

- Promotion tracking (who is getting promoted, and are there patterns of bias?)
- Pay equity audits (ensuring compensation aligns with performance, not personal connections)
- Employee feedback surveys focused on transparency in leadership decisions

If fairness scores are low, leadership coaching and stricter accountability measures should be implemented.

HR is responsible for holding leadership accountable for fostering a workplace culture that prioritizes kindness, fairness, and engagement. However, simply tracking KPIs is not enough—there must be real consequences and incentives tied to leadership behavior.

To ensure kindness remains an organizational priority, HR should:

- Integrate kindness into leadership performance reviews. Leaders should be evaluated not just on business metrics but on how well they engage, support, and develop their teams.
- Tie KPIs to leadership incentives. Managers who excel in engagement and employee satisfaction should receive recognition and tangible rewards.
- Audit HR policies regularly. Workplace policies should reinforce connection, fairness, and psychological safety, not just productivity and efficiency.

By implementing clear KPIs and structured accountability measures, HR ensures that kindness is not just an abstract company value—it is a measurable leadership standard.

When kindness is baked into leadership expectations, employees feel valued, leadership becomes more effective, and retention improves.

The best workplaces are not just successful because of their strategies—they thrive because of their culture. And culture starts with leadership.

Case Study Example: Measuring and Embedding Kindness into Leadership

A midsize tech company had always prided itself on innovation and at-tracting top talent. But over time, leadership noticed a troubling trend—turnover rates were climbing, and employee engagement scores were steadily declining. Employees weren't leaving because of compensation or workload. When HR conducted exit interviews, a clear pattern emerged: Employees didn't feel their managers genuinely cared about their well-being or growth.

One departing employee put it bluntly: "Look, my boss wasn't a bad person. They weren't mean. But they also weren't really present. If I walked in with a problem, they'd nod and say, 'Yeah, that sounds tough,' and move on. After a while, I stopped bringing things up."

Another shared frustration with the lack of meaningful feedback: "The only time my manager gave me any real input was my an-nual review, and even then, it felt like they were reading off a script. I don't need a weekly therapy session, but it would've been nice to know if I was doing a good job before December."

HR dug deeper and found that managerial engagement was incon-sistent across the company. Some teams had highly engaged leaders who regularly checked in with employees, while others had managers who barely spoke outside of project updates. Without a structured approach to leadership engagement, employees in certain teams felt valued and mo-tivated, while others felt invisible.

Taking Action: Measuring and Standardizing Leadership Engagement

Recognizing that kindness couldn't just be left to individual managerial styles, HR and senior leadership launched a *Kindness and Engagement Initiative* designed to make leadership connection measurable, actionable, and a companywide standard.

The first step was launching a quarterly pulse survey focused on lead-ership engagement. Instead of vague questions about workplace satis-faction, employees were asked directly, "How often does your manager check in with you about your well-being and growth?" The results were eye-opening—less than half of employees felt their managers regularly checked in on their development. One employee's response stood out: 'I think my boss assumes that if I'm not complaining, I'm fine. I've had health stuff going on, and I swear they have no idea. Not because I expect them to pry, but because they've never asked."

With data confirming that engagement wasn't just a minor concern but a missing piece of workplace culture, HR developed a structured leadership training program focused on balancing professionalism with genuine connection. Managers participated in workshops where they practiced delivering feedback that was both direct and supportive. They were given strategies for personalizing check-ins without crossing professional boundaries and learned how to ensure fairness and consistency across leadership interactions.

Some managers admitted they had never considered engagement as part of their leadership role. One shared,

I always assumed my team knew I cared because I wasn't yelling at them. But after going through this, I realized just not being a jerk isn't enough. I wasn't actually checking in on them—I was just assuming they were fine until they told me otherwise.

Another manager, initially skeptical, saw the impact firsthand:

I thought this was going to be some corporate fluff, but honestly? It helped. I had a guy on my team who I assumed didn't care about feedback because he's quiet. Turns out, he just didn't know how to ask for it. Now, I make sure to check in, and his work has improved because of it.

HR also tied leadership kindness to measurable KPIs. Managers were expected to conduct regular check-ins that went beyond just project updates, track team engagement trends, and participate in leadership roundtables to share best practices for improving workplace connection. One senior leader who had been resistant to the initiative later admitted,

I used to think leadership was about being efficient, not emotional. Now I get that it's not about having heart-to-hearts every day—it's about making sure people know you actually see them. That's not a waste of time. That's what keeps them here.

The shift toward kindness as a leadership standard was not just anecdotal—it was measurable. Over time, the company saw significant improvements in leadership engagement and employee satisfaction. More employees reported feeling supported by their managers, and turnover among high-performing employees declined.

This transformation was not about forcing leaders to be overly personal or turning the workplace into a social club. It was about ensuring that kindness was embedded in leadership expectations, making employees feel valued, recognized, and engaged.

One employee, who had previously felt disengaged and invisible, described the change:

I don't need my manager to be my best friend, but it's nice to feel like they know I exist. Now, when they ask how I'm doing, I actually believe they want to know.

For years, leadership in the company had relied on outdated assumptions—that employees only cared about paychecks, that performance alone dictated retention, and that emotional intelligence was a secondary skill. But as they incorporated structured leadership training focused on kindness, fairness, and engagement, they saw undeniable results.

By embedding kindness into leadership training and measuring its impact, the company transformed its workplace culture. Employee surveys showed:

- A double-digit increase in trust in leadership, with employees reporting that they felt heard and valued.
- A decrease in voluntary turnover, particularly among top talent who had previously considered leaving.
- A higher rate of employee engagement, with workers feeling more motivated and invested in their roles.

What this experience proved was that kindness in leadership isn't a vague concept—it's a measurable factor that directly influences engagement, retention, and long-term business success.

Companies that dismiss kindness as an intangible, "soft skill" are missing out on one of the most powerful drivers of performance and loyalty. The organizations that recognize kindness as a leadership competency—not just a personality trait—will be the ones that retain top talent, foster innovation, and build sustainable success.

Exercise

Empathy-Building Exercise for Managers: "Know Your Team"

The "Know Your Team" initiative is a structured, yet flexible leadership exercise designed to help managers build meaningful relationships with their teams without crossing professional boundaries. This program encourages leaders to understand their employees beyond just job roles and performance metrics.

Step 1: Gathering Insight—Employee Connection Profiles

- Each employee fills out a brief, voluntary questionnaire with both professional and fun connection questions.

Required Questions (Work Centered):

- What motivates you at work?
- What's one thing you appreciate in a great manager?
- What's a small workplace gesture that makes your day better?
- Do you prefer structured check-ins or more casual interactions?
- Coffee, tea, or neither? Favorite snack?

Optional Fun Connection Questions (For Managers Who Want to Add Personality to Check-Ins):

- What's your favorite movie that came out in the 1980s?
- What's the worst month of the year and why?

- If you could pick one theme song that plays every time you enter a meeting, what would it be?
- What's your ultimate guilty pleasure snack?
- What's a minor inconvenience that irrationally annoys you?

These fun questions add personality to workplace relationships without crossing professional boundaries. Managers can opt to use them when appropriate—some employees may love answering them, while others may prefer to stick to work-related topics.

Step 2: Using Fun Questions to Build Organic Connection

- For informal team meetings—Rotate one fun question at the start of weekly check-ins to lighten the mood and encourage casual conversation.
- For one-on-one check-ins—If an employee mentions loving Reese's Cups, surprising them with one after a tough week is a small gesture that shows thoughtfulness.
- For new employees—Including a mix of work and personal questions in onboarding forms helps managers remember small details that make engagement more natural over time.

Example:

A manager notices that an employee listed "August" as their least favorite month because they hate the heat. When August rolls around, the manager jokes about surviving the worst month together or suggests an iced coffee run to beat the heat. These small, thoughtful moments create genuine connections.

Thought—Adding Personality Without Forcing It:

- Let employees choose what level of engagement feels right for them—some will love these quirky questions, while others may prefer to keep things work-focused.
- Use these insights naturally. A leader who casually references someone's favorite candy or worst month in a lighthearted way demonstrates kindness without being intrusive.

- Keep it fun, not forced. The goal is to create organic interactions, not to turn leadership into a social club.

Step 3: Encouraging Peer-to-Peer Connection

- Managers model teamwide kindness by encouraging employees to participate in structured but low-pressure team engagement.
- Some ideas:
  - "Appreciation Rounds" where employees highlight a teammate's contribution during weekly meetings.
  - "Reverse Mentorship" programs where employees at different levels exchange insights on leadership, work culture, and collaboration.
  - "Team Preferences Wall" (physical or digital) where employees voluntarily list their work style preferences (e.g., "I focus best with headphones on" or "I'm always happy to brainstorm over coffee").

By embedding kindness into leadership training, organizations create a sustainable culture of respect and engagement—one where employees feel genuinely seen, not just managed.

CHAPTER 8

Coaching Leaders to Balance Empathy and Action: Implementing the Pillar of Fairness

Research Insights: Fairness in Leadership—Adapting to Gen Z's Expectations

My research has consistently shown that Gen Z does not passively accept workplace structures—they analyze them, question them, and expect proof that fairness is being upheld. Unlike previous generations, who may have operated under the assumption that hard work will eventually be rewarded, Gen Z wants to know exactly how and when that reward will happen. If transparency is lacking, they are far more likely to disengage— or leave entirely.

One of the most common frustrations among Gen Z employees is unclear career progression. Many have encountered workplaces where promotions feel arbitrary or based on manager discretion rather than structured criteria. Traditional seniority-based advancement, once a valued part of workplace culture, is less appealing to a generation that prioritizes performance, skill development, and clearly defined growth paths. Gen Z is not asking for promotions without merit, but they are demanding a fair and visible system that allows them to see how their efforts translate into career movement.

To address this, companies must rethink their promotion structures and pay transparency. A structured promotion model that includes clear benchmarks, alternative career pathways, and regular performance feedback can help prevent disengagement. My research highlights that organizations with transparent advancement criteria experience higher retention among younger employees because Gen Z is less likely to feel "stuck" in roles without upward mobility.

Similarly, pay secrecy is a major trust killer for Gen Z. Unlike previous generations who may have avoided discussing salary, Gen Z actively compares earnings, researches industry standards, and expects compensation to be both fair and well explained. Organizations that fail to implement clear salary bands, structured raise justifications, and opportunities for skill-based pay growth will struggle to retain Gen Z employees. They are not looking for handouts, but they do expect clarity.

Bias in promotions and compensation is another issue that Gen Z is particularly attuned to. They have grown up in a time where inclusion efforts, pay equity discussions, and bias training are standard conversations. If a company claims to value fairness but fails to show how it actively reduces bias in decision making, Gen Z will see right through it. To combat this, organizations should implement bias checkpoints in promotions, blind resume reviews, and structured performance evaluations based on measurable criteria rather than subjective impressions.

Perhaps most importantly, fairness must be an enforced leadership standard. It cannot be an HR policy that exists on paper but is ignored in practice. Leadership accountability is essential—managers should be evaluated not just on business outcomes but on how fairly they develop, promote, and compensate employees. If an employee is denied a raise or promotion, they should receive a clear, documented explanation along with actionable feedback. Simply avoiding the conversation and hoping they "forget about it" is not a strategy—it's a leadership failure.

A company that successfully adapts to Gen Z's fairness expectations will be one that actively proves its commitment to transparent career growth, pay equity, and bias-free decision making. Organizations that fail to evolve will face higher turnover, lower engagement, and a workforce that is constantly questioning whether leadership actually values fairness—or just says they do.

Practical Implications: Transparency, Career Growth, and Equity in Decision Making

Fairness in leadership isn't about making everyone happy—it's about making sure every employee understands the rules of the game. When career advancement paths, compensation structures, and decision-making processes are clear, employees feel a greater sense of trust in their organization. But fairness is not just about policies; it's about how those policies are communicated and upheld.

One of the biggest mistakes organizations make is assuming fairness means the same thing to everyone. A system that worked for past generations may not resonate with Gen Z. However, fairness does not mean changing company values to suit every preference—it means being transparent about what is valued and how decisions are made so employees can make informed choices about their careers.

Step-by-Step: How Leaders Can Ensure Fairness in Their Organizations

Creating Clear Advancement Paths (Seniority vs. Merit vs. Hybrid Models)

One company I interviewed, a large-scale, regionally known bank, had a clear approach to career advancement: seniority played a significant role. They valued loyalty and believed that those who stayed with the company over time would be rewarded. This wasn't a secret, nor was it disguised behind vague HR language. Employees understood from the beginning that long-term commitment was prioritized over rapid advancement.

An HR leader at the bank explained:

> We don't pretend that we promote based solely on performance. Longevity matters here. If you do your job well and stay with us, you'll be taken care of. That's how we've always done it, and we're upfront about that from the start.

This level of honesty about advancement paths is critical. In previous generations, many employees might have been comfortable with this structure—it offered stability and a sense of long-term security. But for Gen Z, this model can be frustrating.

Gen Z employees tend to prioritize fast growth, skill development, and purpose-driven work. They don't expect promotions to be handed to them, but they do expect clarity on what it takes to move up. The issue isn't necessarily that a company values seniority—it's whether or not that's communicated clearly.

Avoiding the hard truth isn't a leadership strategy, and it certainly isn't kind. Just hoping an employee forgets that they didn't get the promotion or that their bonus was lower than expected isn't fairness—it's avoidance.

One Gen Z employee in my research shared:

I applied for a promotion six months ago. I never got a rejection, just radio silence. Then, one day, I see a new person hired for the role. My manager acted like I'd never even asked. That made me feel stupid for even trying.

Another added: "I'd rather hear no than be left wondering. If I didn't get the job, just tell me. Don't hope I'll forget I asked."

Gen Z doesn't need to be "babied." They just need directness and honesty. If a company values seniority over performance-based promotions, that should be communicated before employees invest years into a system that doesn't align with their expectations.

Organizations can take different approaches to fairness in advancement:

Seniority-Based Model—Rewards loyalty and long-term service. Works well in traditional industries but must be clearly communicated upfront.

Merit-Based Model—Focuses on skills, performance, and results. Appeals more to high-performing, growth-focused employees but must have clear evaluation criteria.

Hybrid Model—Balances experience and performance. May be the best fit for companies wanting to retain institutional knowledge while rewarding innovation and contribution.

Regardless of the model, fairness means making the rules of advancement clear so employees can choose whether that model aligns with their career goals.

Practical Implication: HR's Role in Scaling Fair Leadership

Fairness in leadership cannot be left to chance—it must be structured, measurable, and actively reinforced by HR. When employees feel that career growth, compensation, and workplace decisions are based on transparent, well-defined criteria, they are more engaged, more motivated, and less likely to leave.

HR plays a critical role in ensuring fairness isn't just a leadership value but an operational standard. This includes implementing structured promotion criteria, training leaders on reducing bias, and holding leadership accountable with measurable KPIs.

Fair leadership doesn't happen by accident. It requires structured policies, leadership accountability, and consistent oversight from HR. Without clear systems in place, bias, favoritism, and inconsistent decision making can quietly take hold, eroding trust and engagement.

To make fairness a measurable reality in the workplace, HR must implement policies that reinforce transparency, accountability, and structured decision making.

Require Justification for Pay and Promotion Decisions: HR should implement a standardized documentation system where managers must justify every promotion, pay increase, or major employment decision.

This ensures that:

- Employees understand why certain decisions were made, reducing speculation and mistrust.
- Leadership remains accountable for creating clear, merit-based career advancement opportunities.
- Patterns of bias or unjustified pay gaps can be identified and corrected before they become systemic.

Without structured decision-making transparency, even well-intentioned leadership can appear arbitrary or unfair—which damages employee morale and retention.

Conduct Regular Pay Equity Audits: HR must go beyond one-time statements and actively analyze compensation trends to ensure fairness.

A pay equity audit should assess:

- Salary consistency across gender, race, tenure, and performance.
- Gaps in promotion trends, identifying whether certain employee groups are consistently overlooked.
- Departmental inconsistencies, ensuring that pay structures align with industry benchmarks and internal equity policies.

Organizations that proactively address pay disparities build long-term trust with employees and create a workplace where compensation is seen as fair and justifiable.

Establish an Anonymous Fairness Feedback System: Employees need a structured way to report concerns about fairness without fear of retaliation. HR should implement:

- Anonymized digital feedback channels where employees can raise concerns about favoritism, bias, or unfair treatment.
- Structured response protocols ensuring that complaints are investigated consistently and fairly.
- Regular audits of reported fairness concerns, ensuring that patterns are addressed at the leadership level.

When employees see that fairness concerns are taken seriously, they are more likely to trust leadership and HR processes—leading to higher engagement, retention, and morale.

KPIs for Measuring Fairness in the Workplace

For fairness initiatives to be effective, organizations must track measurable outcomes that reflect equity in leadership decisions, promotions, and workplace policies. These KPIs ensure that fairness is not just an abstract value but an operational priority.

Reduction in Reports of Favoritism or Bias

Perceived favoritism or bias in decision making erodes trust in leadership and fuels disengagement. Regular feedback mechanisms can track whether employees believe their workplace is fair and equitable.

KPI Target: Decrease favoritism-related complaints by 25 percent within a year as reported through HR channels, pulse surveys, or anonymous feedback forms.

Survey Question Example: "I believe promotions and key opportunities in my organization are based on merit rather than personal relationships." (Scale of 1–5)

If favoritism concerns remain high, HR should conduct leadership bias training and implement transparent decision-making processes to address gaps.

Employee Satisfaction with Promotion Processes

A lack of transparency around promotions and career advancement leads to disengagement and turnover. Fairness-driven leadership ensures employees understand how promotions are earned and that opportunities are accessible to all.

KPI Target: Eighty percent of employees report satisfaction with the fairness and transparency of promotions in annual engagement surveys.

HR should track:

- Clarity of promotion criteria in performance reviews
- Employees' perceived fairness of advancement opportunities
- Turnover rates among employees who were overlooked for promotions

If dissatisfaction is high, leadership should hold town halls or Q&A sessions to clarify career progression pathways.

Fair Opportunities for Leadership

Leadership roles should be earned through merit, but organizations also need to ensure that everyone has a fair shot at advancement. It's not just about good intentions—it's about making sure that hard-working employees from all backgrounds can see a path forward.

KPI Target: Aim to grow leadership variety by 15 percent within 2 years so that management better reflects the broader employee base.

To do this, HR should:

- Regularly review promotion data to make sure opportunities are being offered fairly across the company
- Use exit interviews to understand if employees believe leadership paths are open and achievable

If the makeup of leadership isn't changing over time, it's a sign the current system may be limiting growth for some people. In that case, it's time to take a hard look at how promotions are decided and whether the process is truly fair and open to all.

Retention Rates of High-Potential Employees

Fairness is key to retaining top talent. If high-performing employees perceive that leadership decisions are unfair, they are more likely to seek growth opportunities elsewhere.

KPI Target: Reduce voluntary turnover among high-potential employees by 20 percent over 3 years.

HR should analyze:

- Exit interview data for concerns about leadership fairness
- Retention trends among employees identified as high potential
- Impact of fairness policies on employee satisfaction scores

If turnover remains high, organizations must provide clearer career pathways and ensure leadership actively supports employee development.

Transparency in Decision Making

Employees should understand how and why key workplace decisions—such as layoffs, restructuring, or policy changes—are made. A lack of transparency breeds mistrust and disengagement.

KPI Target: Eighty-five percent of employees report that leadership communicates decisions clearly and fairly in internal surveys.

HR should track:

- Employee understanding of leadership decisions in pulse surveys
- Clarity in communication around policy updates
- Effectiveness of leadership Q&A sessions

If transparency scores are low, organizations should implement structured communication frameworks, such as pre-announcement meetings or leadership AMA (Ask Me Anything) sessions.

Pay Equity and Compensation Fairness

Compensation discrepancies erode employee trust and contribute to workplace inequities. Regular pay equity audits ensure fairness in salaries and bonuses.

KPI Target: Conduct annual pay audits to ensure 100 percent alignment between compensation and performance metrics.

HR should measure:

- Pay gaps across roles and demographics
- Consistency in salary adjustments based on performance reviews
- Employee perceptions of pay fairness in engagement surveys

If discrepancies exist, leadership should implement salary transparency policies and structured compensation reviews to address inequities.

Employee Involvement in Policy Changes

Fairness requires employee voice in decision making. If policies are imposed without employee input, they may feel disconnected from leadership and resistant to organizational changes.

KPI Target: Seventy-five percent of employees report feeling heard and involved in workplace policy decisions.

HR should assess:

- Participation rates in feedback sessions or leadership forums
- Effectiveness of policy rollouts based on employee acceptance
- Engagement in companywide discussions on fairness initiatives

If participation is low, organizations should implement structured employee feedback loops and ensure that major decisions include workforce input before finalization.

By implementing clear promotion pathways, bias-reduction training, and fairness-focused KPIs, HR ensures that fairness becomes a leadership standard, not a leadership afterthought. Organizations that embed fairness into their policies will not only build stronger teams—but will also retain their best talent by fostering a workplace where success is truly merit-based.

Case Study Example: Ensuring Pay Transparency and Structured Performance Reviews

One employee from my research captured this frustration vividly: "I worked my ass off last year, and my raise was barely anything. When I asked how they determined it, I got some vague answer about 'economic uncertainty.' Meanwhile, I know for a fact a coworker with less experience got a bigger increase. That didn't help my motivation."

To directly combat this, organizations adopting the Engaged Empathy Leadership Model approach should:

- Make salary bands and promotion criteria public:
  Employees should clearly understand what's required to advance and what compensation ranges they can expect.
- Set structured performance review schedules:
  Annual reviews shouldn't be the only feedback employees receive—regular documented check-ins are critical.
- Provide clear justifications for pay increases:
  Replace vague explanations with transparent demonstrations of how raises, bonuses, and promotions are determined.

Fairness doesn't mean uniform raises or ignoring performance differences. It means every employee understands exactly how the compensation system works and trusts that it's consistently applied.

Case Study Example: Communicating Decisions Openly and Honestly

One of the simplest yet most overlooked aspects of fairness is clear communication. When employees lack understanding of why decisions are made, suspicion grows.

Consider this reflection from an HR manager in my research about a critical mistake during company restructuring:

We pretty much knew layoffs were coming, but leadership told us to keep quiet. They wanted to 'wait until the time was right' to tell employees. What happened instead? Rumors spread like wildfire, panic ensued, and our best employees started jumping ship even before we announced anything. I'll never make that mistake again.

Contrast that scenario with a company that practiced radical transparency:

When a major retailer faced store closures, leadership communicated early and frequently. Employees received advanced notice, relocation options, and direct access to HR support. As a result, employee trust remained intact, and many top performers stayed with the company in new roles.

To foster trust and fairness, organizations should:

- Be transparent about major decisions:
    Clearly explain not just what decisions are made but why they are made.
- Deliver tough news honestly and respectfully:
    Employees prefer difficult truths over unexpected shocks.
- Encourage two-way dialogue:
    Use town halls, regular manager check-ins, or anonymous feedback channels to let employees ask questions and share concerns openly.

Fairness isn't just about the decisions themselves—it's about how those decisions are communicated. Employees don't expect perfect outcomes every time, but they rightly expect honesty and respect.

Exercise

Fairness in Action: A Companywide Exercise: The Fairness Audit—Seeing Through Different Lenses

This interactive companywide exercise is designed to help leadership teams assess fairness in promotions, compensation, and decision making through the eyes of their employees. It combines data-driven insights with real employee experiences to help organizations identify gaps and improve transparency.

Objective:

To evaluate whether employees perceive key workplace policies (promotions, pay, career growth, and decision making) as fair and uncover any hidden gaps in communication, transparency, or execution.

Step 1: The Leadership Fairness Reflection (Pre-Exercise Homework—15 Minutes)

Before the exercise, leaders and HR teams will complete a self-assessment on fairness in the workplace. This should be done individually, without immediate access to employee data.

Questions for Leadership Reflection:

- On a scale of 1 to 5, how fair do you believe our company's promotion process is?
- Are employees fully aware of what is required to advance? How do we ensure they know?
- Do we clearly communicate how pay raises and bonuses are determined?
- What do we think employees would say is the biggest obstacle to career growth here?
- When was the last time a tough decision (promotion, reorganization, pay policy) was explained clearly to employees?

This sets up a baseline perception from leadership before employees provide their feedback.

Step 2: The Employee Fairness Perception Survey (Anonymous—15 Minutes)

Employees complete an anonymous fairness survey, which mirrors the leadership reflection but captures real perceptions from the workforce.

Sample Survey Questions (Scale of 1–5 and Open-Ended Responses):

- I understand what is required to advance in my career at this company.
- The promotion process here feels transparent and fair.

- When I receive a raise, I understand how the decision was made.
- I feel comfortable asking leadership about career growth opportunities.
- What's one thing we could do to improve fairness in promotions or pay?

This provides honest, real-time data on whether employees feel that policies are fair.

Step 3: The Fairness Blind Spot Challenge (Group Discussion—30 Minutes)

Leaders compare their self-assessments to the employee survey results.

- What surprised you? Did leadership rate fairness higher than employees did?
- Where are the biggest gaps? If employees overwhelmingly say they don't understand the promotion process, but leadership assumes they do, this highlights a communication issue.
- What policies need more transparency? If pay raises feel inconsistent to employees, does the company need clearer criteria or better communication about how raises are determined?

This discussion forces leaders to step into their employees' shoes and recognize where gaps in perception and execution exist.

Step 4: Fairness Action Plan (Commitment to Change— 15 Minutes)

Leaders develop a small but concrete action plan based on the results. This could include:

Hosting quarterly "Ask Me Anything" (AMA) sessions on promotions and pay.
Making salary bands and advancement requirements public.

Reworking performance review templates to clarify how employees are evaluated.

Providing employees with structured career growth roadmaps.

Each leadership team commits to one tangible change based on the feedback.

Why This Works:

- Forces leaders to confront potential fairness blind spots.
- Engages employees without making fairness feel like an abstract HR issue.
- Results in a concrete action plan rather than just another "listening session."

CHAPTER 9

Coaching Leaders to Balance Empathy and Action: Implementing the Pillar of Structure

Research Insights: The Impact of Strong Leadership Structures

When expectations are clear, communication is consistent, and policies are transparent, employees don't just feel more secure—they're more engaged, more motivated, and more likely to trust leadership.

My research has shown that Gen Z, in particular, thrives in workplaces where the rules of the game aren't a mystery. They want to know what's expected of them, how to share feedback, and where to find the resources, they need. Without these structures in place, employees are left guessing, second-guessing, and eventually checking out—misinterpreting leadership decisions and losing confidence in the very organization they're supposed to be invested in.

Strong leadership isn't just about being approachable or making good calls in the moment. It's about designing a system that scales—a framework where employees aren't left to figure things out on their own but are given the right tools, guidance, and support to succeed. Because when leadership is structured, success isn't left to chance—it becomes the standard.

A strong leadership structure provides more than just rules—it offers clarity, consistency, and a framework for long-term success. While kindness and fairness in leadership are essential, they cannot thrive without structure. Employees perform best when expectations are clear, communication is frequent, and policies are transparent. Without structure, even the most well-intentioned leaders will find themselves making reactive decisions, struggling with miscommunication, and leaving employees uncertain about their roles and futures.

Gen Z, in particular, values structured workplaces that offer clear expectations and consistent communication. My research shows that lack of clarity is one of the top drivers of disengagement among younger employees. They want to know what's expected of them from the start, how to navigate company policies, and what systems exist to support them. When organizations fail to provide this structure, they risk creating a workplace filled with frustration, confusion, and unnecessary turnover.

Practical Implications: HR's Role in Driving Structure

HR plays a critical role in ensuring that leadership structure is not just an expectation but an operational standard. This means establishing formal leadership development programs, ensuring that company policies align with both business goals and employee engagement, and holding leadership accountable for maintaining structure.

Developing strong leaders requires more than just experience over time—it requires structured, measurable leadership development programs that ensure consistency across departments and align with both business goals and employee engagement. Without clear leadership expectations, organizations risk inconsistent management styles, disengaged employees, and high turnover—especially among Gen Z workers who expect leadership to be structured, fair, and transparent.

KPIs for Structuring Leadership Development and Accountability

Structuring Leadership Development Programs

One of the biggest mistakes organizations make is assuming that leaders will naturally develop over time. In reality, leadership skills must be cultivated, reinforced, and standardized to ensure managers provide consistent, structured leadership across the company.

Gen Z employees, in particular, are highly aware of managerial inconsistencies. They expect that leadership styles will not dramatically shift depending on who their direct supervisor is. If one manager is deeply engaged while another is absent or unclear, trust in leadership erodes. HR must ensure that leadership development is structured, measurable, and aligned with business goals.

Key Actions for HR (Gen Z Adaptations and General Implementation)

- Implement a Leadership Training Roadmap—New and existing managers should follow a structured development program that includes clear milestones for leadership skill-building. This ensures leaders learn standardized communication, feedback, and engagement techniques rather than relying on personal management styles.
- Require Leadership Certification for New Managers—Instead of assuming newly promoted managers know how to lead, require formal training in structured communication, employee engagement, and career development strategies before they begin overseeing teams.
- Ensure Leadership Styles Align Across Departments—Leadership consistency should be monitored through employee feedback to ensure employees experience structured leadership regardless of who they report to. Regular leadership coaching and peer mentorship programs can help maintain alignment.

KPI: Leadership Development Consistency

Increase in Gen Z employees (and workforcewide) reporting that their managers provide clear and consistent expectations, as measured through leadership engagement assessments (target: 85 percent satisfaction or higher).

Reduction in leadership effectiveness gaps across departments, ensuring employees do not experience inconsistent managerial approaches depending on their team.

Ensuring Company Policies Align with Business Goals and Employee Engagement

Company policies should not exist just to check compliance boxes—they should be designed to enhance clarity, drive engagement, and support company performance. Many organizations have policies that are out-dated, unclear, or misaligned with how employees actually work today.

Gen Z, in particular, expects policies to be transparent, accessible, and logical. They are far less likely than previous generations to accept policies "just because that's the way it has always been". My research shows that Gen Z employees are more likely to challenge policies that do not align with business objectives or employee well-being, meaning HR must ensure that policies are clearly communicated, justified, and equitably enforced.

Key Actions for HR (Gen Z Adaptations and General Implementation)

- Conduct a Policy Alignment Audit—Regularly review company policies to ensure they are updated, clear, and directly tied to both business success and employee engagement. If a policy doesn't serve a strategic purpose, it should be revised or eliminated.
- Make Policies Easily Accessible—Policies should not be buried in difficult-to-navigate PDFs or outdated employee handbooks. Instead, they should be stored in interactive platforms (such as an HR portal) where employees can search and reference them easily.
- Ensure Policy Consistency Across Teams—If company policies are not enforced equally across departments, Gen Z employees will quickly identify and call out inconsistencies. HR must regularly audit how policies are implemented to avoid perceptions of unfairness and favoritism.

KPI: Policy Transparency and Accessibility

Reduction in employee-reported confusion over company policies, as measured through HR case tracking and feedback channels (target: 30 percent decrease in policy-related complaints).

Increase in leadership compliance with policy enforcement, ensuring that company rules are fairly and consistently applied across all teams.

Holding Leadership Accountable for Maintaining Structure

HR should not just create policies and leadership programs—it must also enforce them. A structured organization cannot succeed if managers are inconsistent in their execution. Gen Z employees, in particular, expect leadership accountability and will lose trust in an organization if policies are selectively followed or if leadership standards are inconsistently applied.

When leadership accountability is not enforced, employees become frustrated, disengaged, and more likely to leave. Ensuring that managers are held to the same structured leadership expectations across the company prevents this erosion of trust.

Key Actions for HR (Gen Z Adaptations and General Implementation)

- Require Quarterly Leadership Reviews—All managers should be evaluated on their ability to maintain structured leadership, communicate expectations clearly, and uphold company policies. Leadership effectiveness should be measured not only by business performance but also by how well they engage and develop their teams.
- Implement Real-Time Employee Feedback Loops—Employees should be able to anonymously provide feedback on leadership structure and policy execution. If employees feel a policy is being inconsistently enforced, HR should intervene and address the issue.
- Tie Leadership Performance Reviews to Structural Integrity— Managers should not be evaluated solely on business performance metrics—they should also be held accountable for how well they maintain structure within their teams. Fair, consistent leadership should be a core competency in performance reviews.

KPI: Leadership Accountability and Consistency

Reduction in reported leadership inconsistency issues across departments, as measured through HR case tracking and employee feedback (target: 40 percent decrease in leadership-related complaints).

Increase in leadership accountability scores, ensuring that managers are evaluated not just on output but also on their ability to uphold company structure and fairness.

Why Measuring Leadership Structure Matters

Strong leadership development, transparent policies, and leadership accountability drive engagement, trust, and retention. Companies that fail to implement structured leadership frameworks risk high turnover, disengaged employees, and inconsistencies in management styles.

By tracking these KPIs, HR can ensure that:

- Leadership development is structured, measurable, and standardized across the organization.
- Company policies are transparent, fair, and aligned with business success and employee well-being.
- Leaders are held accountable for maintaining structure and consistency, preventing inconsistencies that erode employee trust.

Practical Implications: Step-by-Step—How Leaders Can Create Stronger Structures

Establishing Clear Job Expectations from Day 1

One of the most effective ways to reduce employee frustration is by establishing detailed job expectations from the very beginning. Employees shouldn't have to guess what success looks like in their roles. From onboarding to long-term career growth, a clear structure ensures that employees know what they're responsible for and how they can advance.

A hospitality company I studied successfully implemented quarterly two-way town halls to improve communication and clarify job expectations. These meetings became a game-changer for engagement and transparency. One Gen Z employee shared,

> The amount of information I was able to get from this one town hall was amazing. This town hall focused on the company's expectations surrounding holidays. We are open on holidays, so the employees wanted to know what the structure was. We got incredibly detailed information about who will work when, who will be off when, and how trading holidays works. I have zero questions now.

This level of clarity prevents frustration and last-minute misunderstandings. When employees understand company policies and expectations, they feel more confident in their roles and trust leadership to provide guidance.

Implementing Consistent Communication (Town Halls, Feedback Loops)

Clear structures cannot exist without strong communication channels. Employees need predictable, reliable ways to ask questions, share feedback, and stay informed about company policies. Without structured communication, information becomes inconsistent, scattered, or based on rumors.

Key Communication Strategies for Stronger Leadership Structures:

- Quarterly Two-Way Town Halls: These meetings allow employees to ask leadership direct questions and provide real-time feedback. Transparency increases when employees see leaders respond to concerns in a public, structured forum.
- Regular Team Check-Ins: Instead of waiting for annual reviews, weekly or biweekly team check-ins help maintain alignment on expectations, projects, and concerns.
- Dedicated Feedback Loops: Employees should have multiple ways to share feedback, whether through anonymous surveys, structured one-on-one meetings, or digital platforms.

A structured feedback system ensures employees are heard, issues are addressed, and leaders remain accountable. Gen Z employees, in particular, value ongoing feedback rather than waiting for an annual review to understand how they're performing.

Creating Transparent Policy Handbooks and Making Them Easily Accessible

A lack of easily accessible policies can lead to workplace frustration, misinterpretation, and unnecessary confusion. When employees have to dig through outdated PDFs or ask multiple people for clarification, it creates bottlenecks and slows down efficiency.

A digital learning platform or an internal knowledge base can make company policies clear, searchable, and available at all times. Many workplaces successfully use online training and education platforms to make onboarding, policy updates, and leadership expectations easy to find and digest.

Best Practices for Transparent Policy Handbooks:

- Host Policies on a Centralized Platform: Instead of relying on PDFs, use an interactive, easily searchable knowledge base where employees can quickly find relevant policies.
- Ensure Policies are Written in Clear, Simple Language: Many company handbooks are filled with legal jargon and corporate language that confuses employees. Policies should be concise, direct, and easy to understand.
- Update Policies Based on Employee Feedback: If a policy is consistently misunderstood or causing issues, leaders should be open to revising it for clarity and fairness.

When policies are accessible and easy to navigate, employees spend less time struggling to understand workplace rules and more time focusing on their work assignments.

Case Study Example: How a Hospitality Company Transformed Employee Engagement Through Structure

A midsize hospitality company struggled with high turnover rates and employee uncertainty about career growth. Many employees, particularly younger staff, expressed frustration over unclear expectations, inconsistent leadership, and a lack of structured feedback. The company's existing approach to leadership was largely reactive—managers handled concerns as they arose but failed to proactively communicate expectations or provide consistent guidance.

After analyzing engagement surveys and reviewing exit interview data, leadership realized that the biggest barrier to retention was a lack of structured communication. Employees wanted to know how to advance, what was expected of them, and where they stood in terms of performance. Leadership decided to take a structured, proactive approach to improve workplace engagement, implementing two key changes:

1. Structured Weekly Feedback Sessions—Instead of relying on annual reviews or sporadic check-ins, the company introduced weekly structured feedback sessions for all employees. These short meetings provided clear, actionable feedback on employee performance and professional development opportunities. Employees reported feeling more confident in their roles, less stressed about evaluations, and more engaged in their work.

2. Quarterly Two-Way Town Halls—Leadership created formalized two-way town halls where employees could ask questions and gain clarity on company policies, scheduling expectations, and business goals. These sessions provided an open forum for discussion while maintaining structure, ensuring that leadership directly addressed employee concerns.

The results were significant. Within a year of implementing these structured leadership practices, the company saw:

- A 40 percent increase in employee perceptions of career growth
- A 25 percent improvement in retention
- Higher engagement scores in areas related to clarity, communication, and leadership accountability

One employee summarized the impact: "Before, I felt like I had to figure everything out on my own. Now, I know exactly what's expected of me and what I need to do to grow in my role. It makes a huge difference."

This case highlights a fundamental truth about leadership structure—employees don't just want more feedback, more meetings, or more conversations. They want a structured system that gives them clarity, consistency, and a real path forward. When leaders provide predictability and transparent communication, employees feel more engaged, more secure, and more motivated to stay and grow within the organization.

Exercise

Step-by-Step Manual for Two-Way Town Halls: A Structured Yet Engaging Approach to Workplace Communication

Two-way town halls are one of the most effective ways to bridge the gap between leadership and employees, especially in today's workforce where Gen Z values direct engagement, transparency, and real-time feedback. However, for these town halls to be successful and respected, they must be structured, inclusive, and action-oriented.

This manual outlines a novel, step-by-step approach to implementing two-way town halls that foster genuine dialogue, prevent chaos, and ensure that all employees—whether in person or remote—have their voices heard.

Step 1: Setting the Stage—Scheduling and Accessibility

Town halls should be designed with maximum participation in mind. To ensure that employees across different schedules and locations can attend, HR and leadership should:

- Survey employees in advance to determine the best day, time, and frequency. Some companies may find quarterly meetings work best, while others (such as those in fast-moving industries) may opt for monthly sessions.
- Strongly encourage attendance. While town halls are not mandatory, employees should be given every opportunity to attend live.

- Offer multiple access options. Employees who can't attend in person should be able to join via:
  - Live Zoom or company video platform
  - FaceTime or another quick-call option (Gen Z is comfortable joining through a friend's phone)
  - A recorded version available afterward for those who absolutely cannot join
- Create a standing annual or quarterly schedule so employees can plan ahead and integrate it into their work routines.

Step 2: Structuring the Agenda—No Free-for-Alls

To keep the discussion productive and fair, all employees who wish to ask a question or provide input should submit their name in advance.

- Employees submit their questions or comments ahead of time via an internal form, Slack thread, or e-mail. This ensures the town hall stays focused and organized.
- A running list is displayed during the meeting, so employees know whose turn it is. This prevents random shouting or back-and-forth arguments that derail the discussion.
- Employees can still add their name to the list during the meeting, but no off-the-cuff shouting will be allowed—this maintains professionalism and ensures fairness.

This structure gives every voice a chance to be heard, while avoiding the chaos of unstructured, reactive discussions.

Step 3: Facilitating the Meeting—The Right Balance of Leadership and Employee Voices

A designated moderator (HR, a senior leader, or a rotating facilitator) will guide the discussion, ensuring:

- Each employee gets a fair and uninterrupted opportunity to speak when it's their turn.

- Leadership actively listens and does not just respond defensively. The goal is to engage in meaningful dialogue, not dismiss concerns.
- Key points are recorded and visible (on a shared document, screen, or whiteboard) so employees know their comments are being taken seriously.

To increase engagement and energy, town halls can integrate quick interactive moments, such as:

- Live Polls—Employees can vote on key issues in real time (e.g., Would you rather receive bonuses based on performance metrics or team-based goals?)
- Mini Breakout Sessions—If a major issue arises (such as new workplace policies), small teams can briefly discuss and present insights back to leadership.
- A "Wildcard" Spot—While structured, leave one open slot for a last-minute topic employees can vote on discussing at the end.

This balance keeps the meeting structured yet flexible and prevents monotony.

Step 4: The Closing Ritual—Management Takes a Turn

To ensure town halls do not feel like a one-way interrogation of leadership, the session should end with leadership asking employees questions.

- "What's one thing we're doing well that we should keep?"
- "If you could change one thing about how we communicate as a company, what would it be?"
- "What's something we aren't thinking about that we should be?"

This flips the power dynamic, showing that leadership is not just responding but also actively seeking employee insights.

Finally, before closing, leadership should summarize key action items that emerged from the discussion, ensuring:

- Employees know what will be followed up on
- They understand what leadership will do next
- There is accountability for what was discussed

Step 5: Post-Town Hall Follow-Up—Turning Words into Action

To prevent town halls from becoming just another corporate meeting, leadership must demonstrate real accountability after each session.

- Send out a recap of key discussion points within 48 hours, highlighting:
  - Employee concerns discussed
  - Leadership's responses
  - Next steps and timelines for any promised actions
- If certain issues require additional review, a follow-up deadline should be set so that employees don't feel their concerns were dismissed.
- Recognize employees who contributed thoughtful feedback (without singling out negative comments).

A feedback survey should also be sent out after the town hall, asking:

- Did you feel this meeting was productive?
- Did you feel your concerns were heard?
- Would you like to suggest topics for the next town hall?

Why This Town Hall Structure Works

- Ensures fairness and prevents the loudest voices from dominating
- Encourages real participation across all employees (remote, in-person, different shifts)

- Provides structure while allowing flexibility
- Ends with leadership taking an active role in learning from employees
- Turns employee feedback into measurable action

This structured yet dynamic approach to two-way town halls creates a real culture of engagement. Employees feel heard, leadership remains accountable, and the company fosters an environment where open dialogue isn't just encouraged—it's expected.

Final Thoughts: Leadership Is Not Passive

The Engaged Empathy Leadership Model (EELM) is not a passive concept—it is an active, intentional approach to leadership that requires consistent effort and accountability. It's not enough for leaders to simply mean well or have good intentions. Strong leadership is measured by actions, not assumptions.

Too many organizations assume that a positive workplace culture will happen organically—that as long as leaders are generally supportive, employees will remain engaged. But leadership without structure, fairness, and accountability leads to inconsistency, disengagement, and ultimately, turnover.

Great leadership isn't about being "nice" or making employees happy all the time—it's about ensuring that people feel valued, respected, and set up for success.

When kindness, fairness, and structure are embedded into leadership practices, organizations see:

- Stronger workplace cultures, where employees feel connected and engaged.
- Higher retention rates, as employees trust leadership and see a future in the company.
- More effective teams, because expectations, opportunities, and support are clear.

Leadership Must Be Proactive, Not Reactive

Organizations often wait until problems arise—low engagement, high turnover, declining performance—before they start addressing leadership issues. But reactive leadership is already too late. Employees don't disengage overnight; they disengage over time when they feel unheard, undervalued, or unsupported.

Instead, leadership must be proactive:

- Kindness must be intentional. Engagement doesn't happen by accident—leaders must actively create opportunities for employees to feel recognized, appreciated, and heard.
- Fairness must be built into decision making. Employees don't expect every outcome to go their way, but they do expect transparency and consistency in how leadership decisions are made.
- Structure must provide clarity and stability. Without clear expectations, career paths, and performance standards, even the most talented employees will struggle to thrive.

The future of leadership isn't about eliminating authority or making work easy—it's about leading with clarity and purpose.

The organizations that get this right will be the ones that:

- Develop leaders at every level—ensuring that leadership isn't just a title but a skill set built on engagement and accountability.
- Retain top talent—by fostering an environment where employees see fair opportunities for growth and development.
- Adapt to the future of work—embracing flexibility, technology, and generational leadership shifts without losing structure.

Great leadership doesn't happen by default—it happens by design. Organizations that prioritize intentional leadership will not just survive the changing workplace—they will define it.

CHAPTER 10

How Companies That Implement EELM Are Seeing Results

Several organizations that participated in my research tested the EELM model and tracked key leadership outcomes.

Case Study 1: How a Tutoring Company Transformed Employee Engagement with Casual Check-Ins

The Problem: High Turnover and Disengaged Employees

A midsize tutoring company was facing an alarming rate of employee turnover. Despite offering competitive pay and flexible scheduling, the company struggled to retain its tutors—primarily Gen Z professionals. Many left before reaching their 1-year anniversary, forcing the company into a continuous cycle of hiring and retraining.

The underlying issue wasn't compensation or job flexibility—it was a lack of connection between leadership and employees. Tutors reported feeling like temporary, replaceable workers rather than valued members of the team. Leadership only engaged with employees during performance reviews or administrative meetings, leaving little room for genuine human interaction.

Exit interviews consistently pointed to the same problem: Tutors weren't leaving for better pay; they were leaving because they didn't feel recognized, supported, or connected to leadership.

The Solution: Introducing Casual One-on-One Check-Ins

Rather than implementing a rigid performance management system, leadership took a different approach—regular, informal check-ins designed to foster genuine connection.

Supervisors committed to meeting with each tutor every few weeks in a relaxed setting. Whether it was a quick conversation after a session, a coffee chat, or a short walk, these check-ins weren't about metrics or evaluations. They were about building relationships and making employees feel seen.

Leaders were encouraged to:

- Ask employees about their experiences—what was working, what wasn't, and how they felt about their roles.
- Show genuine interest in employees as individuals, not just as workers.
- Provide mentorship and career guidance when appropriate.

One tutor summed up the impact: "Before these check-ins, I felt like I was just another name on the schedule. Now, my supervisor knows my career goals, checks in on my progress, and actually listens to my feedback. I feel like I matter here."

The Results: A Noticeable Shift in Retention and Engagement

Within 6 months, the company saw measurable improvements in both retention and employee satisfaction:

- Retention increased by 18 percent, with fewer tutors leaving within their first year.
- Employee satisfaction improved by 22 percent, as measured by internal surveys.
- Higher participation in company initiatives, with more tutors attending optional training sessions and team meetings.

Leaders found that these small, intentional moments of connection had a profound effect. What had once felt like a transactional work environment became a more collaborative and supportive space.

The Leadership Lesson: Engagement Doesn't Require Grand Gestures

Many organizations assume that boosting engagement requires costly initiatives, large-scale leadership training, or extravagant perks. But this case study demonstrates that simple, consistent leadership habits—like casual check-ins—can transform workplace culture.

For leaders looking to improve engagement, retention, and trust within their teams, the takeaway is clear: show up, listen, and connect. Employees don't just want a paycheck—they want to feel valued, heard, and supported.

Questions for Thought and Discussion

1. Leadership and Engagement: How can leaders ensure that engagement efforts feel genuine rather than performative?
2. Retention Strategies: What other low-cost, high-impact strategies could companies implement to reduce turnover beyond casual check-ins?
3. Personalization in Leadership: How can managers tailor engagement efforts to fit different employee personalities and communication styles?
4. Measuring Impact: What key performance indicators (KPIs) should organizations track to determine if their engagement initiatives are working?
5. Scalability: How can larger organizations implement similar engagement strategies without overwhelming managers with additional responsibilities?
6. Generational Expectations: How do Gen Z's expectations for leadership and workplace culture differ from previous generations, and how should companies adapt?
7. Employee–Manager Relationships: What are the risks of informal check-ins, and how can leaders balance casual engagement with maintaining professional boundaries?
8. Organizational Buy-In: How can HR and senior leadership encourage middle managers to adopt a more engaged leadership approach?
9. Long-Term Sustainability: What steps can companies take to ensure that engagement strategies like these remain effective as the organization grows and evolves?
10. Cultural Impact: How does a culture of frequent, informal check-ins affect overall workplace morale, and what potential downsides should be considered?

Case Study 2: How a Production Company Shifted from Seniority-Based Promotions to Merit-Driven Rewards

The Problem: Employee Frustration Over Promotion and Recognition

A midsize production company was facing growing discontent among its workforce. Promotions and bonuses had long been awarded based on tenure rather than performance, innovation, or leadership potential. While this seniority-based system had worked in the past, it was clear that it no longer met the expectations of a changing workforce—particularly among Gen Z and millennial employees.

Younger employees voiced increasing frustration over the lack of transparency in career advancement. Many felt that no matter how hard they worked or how much they contributed, they would always be passed over in favor of employees who had simply been there longer. This led to declining motivation, strained collaboration between teams, and the departure of high-potential employees seeking workplaces where effort and impact were rewarded.

One employee summed it up candidly:

> I love my job, but it feels like it doesn't matter how well I perform. The next promotion will go to whoever has been here the longest, not who's actually making the biggest impact.

Exit interviews confirmed this frustration. Employees weren't leaving because of pay—they were leaving because they saw no path forward. Leadership recognized that if they didn't modernize their approach to promotions and incentives, they would continue losing their most talented and driven employees.

The Solution: Restructuring Bonuses to Reward Team Outcomes

Rather than immediately dismantling the existing promotion system, leadership took a phased approach by first restructuring how bonuses were awarded. The new system focused on recognizing measurable contributions and collaborative success rather than tenure alone.

Key changes included:

- Performance-Based Bonuses: Bonuses were now tied to project success, innovation, and measurable contributions rather than simply years of service.
- Team-Oriented Rewards: Cross-functional collaboration was encouraged by rewarding entire teams for shared achievements, fostering a culture of cooperation rather than competition.
- Clear Advancement Criteria: Employees were given a transparent framework outlining how contributions would be evaluated and how they could qualify for bonuses.

A senior manager described the shift: "Before, promotions and bonuses felt automatic, tied to tenure instead of talent. Now, employees are engaged because they know their efforts actually make a difference in how they're rewarded."

The Results: A Major Boost in Team Collaboration and Engagement

Within the first year of implementing the new system, the company saw:

- A 30 percent increase in interdepartmental collaboration, as employees were now motivated to work across teams to achieve shared goals.
- Higher engagement in leadership roles, as employees took on greater responsibilities knowing their efforts would be fairly recognized.
- Lower turnover among high-potential employees, as they saw a clear, merit-based path to career advancement.

The cultural impact was just as significant as the business results. Employees who had previously felt overlooked were now more engaged in problem-solving, teamwork, and leadership. Motivation surged as employees realized that their hard work and contributions would no longer go unnoticed.

The Leadership Lesson: Fair Recognition Creates Engagement

This case study highlights a crucial leadership insight: When employees feel like their contributions truly matter, they perform at a higher level.

Many organizations assume that seniority-based systems foster loyalty, but in reality, they often lead to stagnation and disengagement. High-performing employees become frustrated when their impact is not acknowledged, leading them to seek opportunities elsewhere. By shifting toward a merit-based incentive structure, this company was able to motivate employees without completely dismantling existing structures.

For leaders looking to increase engagement and collaboration, the takeaway is clear: recognition should be tied to effort and impact, not just tenure. When employees believe that hard work leads to tangible rewards, they are far more likely to stay, contribute, and push the organization forward.

Questions for Thought and Discussion

1. Leadership and Recognition: How can companies balance the need for structure with the flexibility required to recognize top performers?
2. Employee Motivation: What are the potential risks of merit-based promotions, and how can organizations ensure fairness in implementation?
3. Cultural Shifts: How can long-standing companies transition from seniority-based systems to performance-driven rewards without creating resistance among veteran employees?
4. Measuring Impact: What metrics should organizations use to ensure that merit-based incentives are truly rewarding the right behaviors?
5. Retention Strategies: Beyond financial incentives, what other strategies can organizations use to retain high-potential employees who feel overlooked?
6. Generational Perspectives: How do different generations perceive fairness in promotions, and how can leaders address these expectations effectively?

7. Scalability: How can large organizations implement similar reward systems without creating excessive competition or resentment among employees?

8. Transparency in Decision Making: How can leadership communicate changes in promotion and bonus structures to gain buy-in from employees at all levels?

9. Long-Term Success: What steps should organizations take to ensure that merit-based systems remain fair, consistent, and free of bias over time?

10. Team Versus Individual Recognition: What are the advantages and challenges of rewarding team performance versus individual contributions, and how can organizations strike the right balance?

Case Study 3: How a Hospitality Business Increased Retention with Quarterly Town Halls

The Problem: No Clear Career Growth Pathway

A hospitality company operating multiple locations was facing a persistent challenge—high turnover rates, particularly among younger employees. The issue wasn't related to wages, benefits, or workplace culture. Instead, employees felt uncertain about their future within the company. Without a clear career growth pathway, many saw their roles as temporary rather than opportunities for long-term advancement.

Frustration was widespread among staff. Promotions and internal mobility felt arbitrary, with no transparent criteria outlining how employees could move up. Leadership rarely communicated expectations for career progression, leaving employees in the dark about what skills, performance milestones, or tenure were required for advancement.

One employee expressed the frustration directly: "I love working here, but I have no idea how to move up. Who decides promotions? What do I need to do to be considered? It's like a mystery."

This lack of transparency led to disengagement, low morale, and turnover—particularly among Gen Z employees, who expect clear communication about growth opportunities. If employees didn't see a future within the company, they were quick to seek roles elsewhere.

The Solution: Implementing Quarterly Two-Way Town Halls

Instead of relying on annual reviews or sporadic one-on-one check-ins, leadership introduced quarterly town halls designed to foster open, structured communication between employees and management.

The goal was to:

- Clarify career advancement opportunities by outlining specific skills, performance metrics, and milestones required for promotions.
- Encourage employees to ask questions and voice concerns in a safe, structured environment.
- Increase leadership transparency by openly discussing company policies, workplace changes, and strategic goals.
- Strengthen trust between employees and management by demonstrating that leadership was actively listening and responding to concerns.

To ensure effectiveness, the company established clear guidelines for these town halls:

- Employees were encouraged to submit questions in advance so that leadership could provide well-prepared, thoughtful responses.
- Sessions were recorded so that employees who couldn't attend could still benefit from the discussions.
- Post-town hall surveys were conducted to gauge effectiveness and gather input for future sessions.
- A designated facilitator moderated discussions, ensuring that all voices were heard rather than allowing a few dominant voices to control the conversation.

The results were immediate. Employees who had previously felt disconnected from leadership now had a direct channel to get answers. One Gen Z employee described how impactful the first session was:

The amount of information I got from just one town hall was incredible. We talked about holiday scheduling policies, how promotions work, and how we can trade shifts in a way that's fair. I have zero questions now—everything was laid out clearly.

The Results: A Shift in Career Growth Perception and Retention

Within a year of implementing quarterly town halls, the company experienced measurable improvements:

- A 40 percent increase in career growth perception, as employees gained clarity on how they could advance within the company.
- A 25 percent improvement in retention, as fewer employees left due to uncertainty about their future.
- More employees proactively seeking leadership roles, signaling an increase in long-term investment in the company.

Perhaps the most significant outcome was the cultural shift toward transparency and trust. Employees no longer felt like they were left in the dark about promotions, pay, and company policies. Instead, they felt heard, valued, and informed—which directly impacted their motivation to stay and grow within the company.

The Leadership Lesson: Transparency is a Powerful Retention Tool

This case study reinforces a key leadership truth: Employees don't just need career opportunities—they need to understand how to achieve them.

Many businesses unknowingly lose top talent not because there are no pathways for growth, but because leadership fails to communicate them clearly. Employees who feel uncertain about their future within an organization will inevitably start looking elsewhere.

Companies that prioritize structured, two-way communication—whether through town halls, regular check-ins, or open forums—will retain engaged employees who see a clear future within the company. Those that continue to operate with vague leadership communication and unclear advancement pathways will struggle with disengagement and high turnover.

For leaders, the takeaway is clear: When employees know what to expect, they don't just stay—they invest.

Questions for Thought and Discussion

1. Leadership Transparency: How can organizations ensure that career advancement opportunities are clearly communicated at all levels?
2. Employee Engagement: What are the risks of not providing structured forums for employees to ask questions and voice concerns?
3. Trust in Leadership: How does transparency in leadership impact employee retention and morale?
4. Career Progression: What specific strategies can businesses implement to ensure employees understand their career growth opportunities?
5. Generational Expectations: How do Gen Z employees' expectations for workplace communication differ from previous generations?
6. Measuring Effectiveness: What key performance indicators (KPIs) should companies use to track the impact of leadership transparency initiatives?
7. Scaling Transparency: How can large organizations maintain structured communication when managing thousands of employees across multiple locations?
8. Preventing Information Overload: How can leadership balance transparency with providing relevant, actionable information without overwhelming employees?
9. Beyond Town Halls: What other methods can companies use to encourage open dialogue between employees and management?
10. Long-Term Success: How can businesses ensure that town halls and other transparency efforts remain effective over time rather than becoming routine, uninspired meetings?

Case Study 4: How a Tech Company Increased Engagement, Fairness, and Structure with EELM

The Problem: A Fast-Growing Company Struggling with Employee Retention

A rapidly expanding tech company had built a strong reputation for innovation, competitive salaries, and an exciting work environment. However, despite these advantages, they faced a growing problem—employee retention.

Exit interviews revealed that employees weren't leaving due to compensation or workload but because they felt disconnected from leadership, unsure about career advancement, and frustrated by perceived favoritism.

Common complaints included:

- Lack of engagement—Employees felt leadership was too distant and only interacted with them in formal meetings.
- Unclear promotion paths—Many employees didn't know what it took to advance, leading to disengagement and frustration.
- Perceived favoritism—"Big voices" dominated decision making, and quieter high performers often felt overlooked.
- Unstructured leadership development—Employees who wanted to grow into leadership roles weren't sure how to get there.

One employee summed up the frustration:

I don't mind working hard, but I feel like leadership only notices the people who speak the loudest. I have no idea what I need to do to move up, and there's no clear guidance on how decisions are made.

The Solution: Implementing Engaged Empathy Leadership Model (EELM) with a Three-Pillar Approach

Recognizing that small, isolated changes wouldn't solve the problem, the company's leadership team decided to take a comprehensive approach by incorporating all three pillars of Engaged Empathy Leadership Model (EELM): Kindness, Fairness, and Structure.

Kindness: Building Personal Connections Through Intentional Check-Ins

The leadership team introduced weekly 5-minute stand-ups where managers checked in with employees—not just about projects but about their overall well-being and job satisfaction. These were informal and designed to foster genuine human connection.

Additionally, the company launched monthly digital happy hours, peer recognition programs, and an annual Secret Santa exchange to build a stronger team culture—even in a hybrid work environment.

A manager who had initially been skeptical of these efforts later admitted: "At first, I thought this was just feel-good stuff. But now, I actually know my team better. When employees feel like you see them as people, not just workers, they stay longer and perform better."

Fairness: Creating Transparency in Promotions and Performance Reviews

To address perceived favoritism and lack of clarity around promotions, HR implemented a structured, transparent career advancement framework.
This included:

- A documented promotion pathway, outlining specific performance milestones, skills, and leadership qualities required for advancement.
- Anonymous fairness feedback surveys, where employees could raise concerns about bias in promotions or pay decisions.
- Structured performance reviews, ensuring that leadership decisions were based on measurable contributions rather than personal relationships.

Employees immediately noticed the difference. One software engineer who had previously considered leaving shared: "Before, I felt like promotions were a mystery. Now, I know exactly what I need to do to get to the next level. Even if I don't get promoted right away, I at least understand why and what I need to improve."

Structure: Leadership Training and Defined Growth Opportunities

To create clearer leadership pathways, the company developed a dual-track leadership model, allowing employees to grow as either:

1. People leaders (focused on managing teams).
2. Expert leaders (focused on innovation and technical mastery).

Managers were also required to complete leadership development training, ensuring they understood how to balance kindness, fairness, and structure in their leadership approach.

Additionally, the company:

- Launched quarterly town halls to improve leadership transparency.
- Encouraged managers to rotate meeting facilitators, preventing dominant voices from controlling discussions.
- Implemented structured mentorship programs, ensuring employees who wanted leadership roles had a clear development plan.

One Gen Z employee described the impact of these changes: "I was considering leaving because I felt stuck. Now, I know my company is investing in me. There's a clear path forward, and my manager actually checks in with me about it."

The Results: A Stronger, More Engaged Workforce

Within the first year of implementing EELM, the company saw measurable improvements:

- A 35 percent drop in voluntary turnover, especially among high-potential employees.
- A 40 percent increase in employee engagement scores, with higher participation in town halls and feedback sessions.
- A more diverse leadership pipeline, as employees who previously felt overlooked were now advancing based on merit, not visibility.

Additionally, managers reported fewer daily frustrations, as clearer expectations and structured leadership development reduced confusion and workplace tensions.

The Leadership Lesson: Engagement, Fairness, and Structure Work Together

This case study demonstrates that leadership issues are rarely solved with just one fix.

- Kindness builds personal connection and trust in leadership.
- Fairness ensures all employees feel valued and recognized.
- Structure provides clarity and stability, preventing uncertainty.

By addressing all three elements together, the company transformed its leadership culture, reduced turnover, and strengthened its talent pipeline.

Questions for Thought and Discussion

1. Leadership Engagement: How can managers ensure they engage with all employees, not just the most vocal ones?
2. Promotion Transparency: What strategies can organizations use to make career growth pathways clearer?
3. Avoiding Favoritism: How can leadership prevent bias in promotions, raises, and opportunities?
4. Employee Retention: How do structured career development programs impact retention and engagement?
5. Remote and Hybrid Work Challenges: What additional steps can companies take to ensure fairness and engagement in hybrid or remote settings?
6. Balancing People and Expert Leadership: How can organizations create leadership opportunities for employees who may not want to manage people?
7. Measuring Success: What key performance indicators (KPIs) should be tracked to ensure leadership strategies are working?
8. Long-Term Impact: How can companies ensure that engagement efforts remain consistent rather than fading over time?
9. Scaling Leadership Development: What are the best ways to implement structured leadership training at scale?
10. Employee Buy-In: How can leadership ensure employees see changes as genuine rather than performative?

Final Takeaway: The Data Is Clear—Leadership Must Adapt

The research is undeniable: kindness, fairness, and structure are not just "nice-to-haves" in leadership—they are the foundation of high-performing, engaged workplaces. Organizations that prioritize leadership engagement retain top talent, reduce turnover, and outperform those that rely on outdated, rigid leadership models.

The reality is stark—companies that fail to evolve will lose Gen Z employees to organizations that embrace transparency, structure, and authentic leadership. This generation doesn't just ask for better leadership; they expect it. And they're willing to leave if they don't get it.

A 2022 Gallup study found that organizations with highly engaged employees experience 23 percent higher profitability and 18 percent less turnover than those with low engagement levels. Another report from the *Harvard Business Review* revealed that employees who feel their managers communicate transparently are 47 percent more likely to stay with their company. These statistics highlight a crucial truth: engaged leadership isn't just about making employees feel good—it's a direct driver of business success.

The Engaged Empathy Leadership Model (EELM) is not just a theory—it is a research-backed strategy that works. Studies on leadership effectiveness confirm that a combination of empathy, fairness, and structure leads to higher productivity, stronger team cohesion, and improved retention rates. Leaders who prioritize fairness and structured decision making reduce workplace bias, foster trust, and create a more stable work environment.

Companies that embrace these principles won't just build stronger teams; they'll create workplaces where employees want to grow, innovate, and lead. They will future-proof their leadership models, setting the foundation for long-term success in an evolving workforce.

Key Takeaways from Part 3: Implementing Engaged Empathy Leadership Model (EELM)

Engaged Empathy Leadership Model (EELM) is not just a concept—it's a leadership model that drives real business impact. Leaders who apply kindness, fairness, and structure create workplaces where employees feel valued, engaged, and motivated to perform at their best.

Kindness: More Than a Soft Skill—A Leadership Strategy

- Kindness in leadership fosters trust, psychological safety, and employee commitment.

- Employees who feel valued by leadership are more likely to stay engaged and loyal to an organization.
- True kindness is actionable—it goes beyond being "nice" to creating an environment where employees feel seen and supported in meaningful ways.
- Casual check-ins, personal recognition, and authentic engagement strengthen relationships between leaders and their teams.

Fairness: Eliminating Bias and Building Trust

- Employees don't need to agree with every decision, but they must trust the decision-making process.
- Transparency in promotions, raises, and opportunities fosters workplace trust.
- Leaders who fail to address perceptions of favoritism or inconsistency will lose credibility.
- Establishing clear policies and structured leadership training helps ensure fairness is consistently applied across teams.

Structure: Clarity Drives Performance

- Employees thrive in environments where expectations, responsibilities, and career growth pathways are clearly defined.
- Structure does not mean rigidity—it means creating an intentional framework where employees know what success looks like.
- Gen Z, in particular, expects structured leadership and transparent decision-making processes.
- Without structure, kindness and fairness lose their effectiveness—leading to disengagement, frustration, and high turnover.

How EELM Improves Retention and Engagement

- Organizations with leaders who actively engage employees see higher productivity, lower turnover, and stronger overall performance.

- Gen Z and millennial employees are particularly drawn to workplaces where fairness, career progression, and leadership accountability are prioritized.
- Leadership must be measurable—clear KPIs should track fairness in promotions, engagement levels, and leadership consistency.

Final Thought: Leadership That Works

Engaged Empathy Leadership Model is about balancing human connection with strategic leadership.

- Leaders must engage rather than passively listen.
- Employees must feel safe but also challenged to grow.
- Kindness, fairness, and structure are nonnegotiable elements of effective leadership.

Organizations that adopt EELM will outperform competitors, retain top talent, and foster workplaces where people don't just work—they thrive.

PART 4

The Future of Leadership

CHAPTER 11

The Future of the Engaged Empathy Leadership Model (EELM)

As leadership continues to evolve, the Engaged Empathy Leadership Model (EELM) will adapt to new workforce expectations, technological advancements, and shifts in organizational structures. The core pillars of Kindness, Fairness, and Structure remain essential, but how they are implemented will evolve alongside new leadership challenges.

Kindness Will Expand Beyond Individual Leadership to Organizational Culture

Historically, kindness in leadership has been seen as a personal leadership trait—something an individual leader brings to their team. Moving forward, kindness will need to be embedded at an organizational level through structured policies, companywide well-being initiatives, and leadership training that emphasizes emotional intelligence at all levels.

Future of Kindness in Leadership:

- Beyond the leader: Kindness will not just be a leadership style but a companywide value embedded into hiring, performance management, and employee well-being programs.
- Technology and kindness: AI and automation will change how leaders interact with employees—leaders must ensure that technology supports, rather than replaces, human connection.
- Emotional intelligence as a leadership standard: Future leadership development programs will need to prioritize EQ (emotional intelligence) as much as business acumen.

Fairness Will Be Driven by Transparency and Real-Time Feedback

Fairness in leadership is no longer just about pay and promotions—it's about trust. Employees, particularly Gen Z and future generations, expect radical transparency in how decisions are made.

Future of Fairness in Leadership:

- Data-driven fairness: Organizations will rely more on analytics and AI-driven insights to detect bias in hiring, promotions, and pay decisions.
- Real-time performance evaluation: Traditional annual reviews will become obsolete. Instead, companies will implement continuous performance feedback loops to ensure employees always know where they stand.
- Fairness audits will be the norm: Businesses will regularly assess fairness metrics across departments to identify disparities before they become systemic issues.

Structure Will Evolve to Balance Flexibility with Accountability

The biggest challenge in future leadership will be balancing the need for structure with employees' desire for flexibility. The EELM model will remain critical in helping companies create clear, fair, and transparent leadership structures while allowing employees to thrive in fluid work environments.

Future of Structure in Leadership:

- AI-driven leadership support: Leaders will use AI-powered dashboards to track employee engagement, communication trends, and leadership effectiveness in real time.
- Hybrid leadership structures: Companies will develop leadership models that blend hierarchical decision making with decentralized, team-driven leadership.

- Standardized leadership expectations: Companies will create universal leadership training and accountability metrics to ensure employees receive consistent leadership, no matter their department or manager.

As Gen Z moves into leadership and Gen Alpha begins entering the workforce, the principles of Kindness, Fairness, and Structure will remain critical, but their application will evolve.

Kindness will be measured at an organizational level, not just a leadership level.

Fairness will be increasingly data-driven, ensuring bias-free decision making.

Structure will need to balance flexibility with clear expectations and accountability.

The organizations that apply these evolving principles will retain top talent, foster trust, and remain competitive in the future workforce.

CHAPTER 12

Gen Z as Leaders and Predictions for Gen Alpha

As Gen Z transitions into leadership roles, my research shows that they are redefining what it means to be a leader. Leadership is no longer just about authority and hierarchy—it's about influence, trust, and expertise. While previous generations viewed leadership as a top-down structure, Gen Z sees it as collaborative, flexible, and focused on enabling teams to succeed.

This shift does not mean leadership will disappear. Instead, leadership will evolve into a dual-track system:

- People leaders—Traditional managers who focus on developing teams, coaching employees, and aligning company culture.
- Expert leaders—Highly skilled individual contributors who lead through specialized knowledge, driving key projects and innovations without necessarily managing direct reports.

This distinction is critical because my research shows that Gen Z values expertise just as much as managerial authority. Employees should not have to climb the management ladder to be considered a leader—they can lead through knowledge, problem-solving, and project ownership.

Research Insights: Leadership as an Enabler, Not a Taskmaster

My research consistently finds that Gen Z leaders do not equate leadership with control. Instead, they focus on empowering teams, removing obstacles, and providing strategic clarity.

One participant described their vision for leadership:

It's hard to imagine, but I think my leadership style will ultimately be hands-off when it comes to the actual work of analysis, forecasting, and execution. Instead, I see my role as enabling my team to do that work effectively—communicating progress, establishing data flows, and setting expectations they can achieve. What I don't want to become is the kind of manager who can't let go of the details I used to handle myself. That stifles a team and ultimately becomes counterproductive.

This aligns with my research findings that Gen Z leaders favor autonomy and trust over micromanagement. They are far less likely to interfere in day-to-day tasks and more likely to focus on:

- Providing clear expectations and goals
- Creating efficient systems and communication flows
- Encouraging employees to take ownership of their work

A Consensus: The Future of Leadership Will Be More Flexible Yet Structured

Leadership is not disappearing—it's evolving. My research shows that Gen Z leaders are not rejecting structure—they are redefining it to create a more effective and sustainable model for the modern workplace.

They still value clear expectations, accountability, and leadership development, but they reject rigid, outdated leadership models that rely on hierarchy, bureaucracy, and top-down control.

The emerging consensus among Gen Z leaders is that the best workplaces of the future will blend flexibility with structure by:

- Establishing clear but adaptable organizational frameworks that provide stability without rigidity. Employees should know their roles, responsibilities, and career paths—but also feel empowered to challenge, refine, and innovate within those structures.

- Distributing leadership so that employees with expertise can lead projects, initiatives, and innovations—without requiring a formal management title. Leadership will no longer be solely tied to hierarchy but will be based on contribution and influence.
- Encouraging leaders to act as facilitators and enablers, rather than decision-making gatekeepers. Instead of dictating every move, the best leaders will create environments where teams have the resources, autonomy, and support needed to succeed.
- Measuring success through engagement, collaboration, and innovation—not just output. Productivity alone will no longer be the primary measure of success. The workplaces of the future will also value employee engagement, knowledge-sharing, and the ability to adapt to new challenges.

One Gen Z leader I interviewed summed up this shift perfectly: "I don't think we'll be turning everything upside down, but leadership will look different. We'll see more influence-based leadership rather than hierarchy-driven leadership. The best leaders won't be the ones who control everything, but the ones who make sure their teams have everything they need to succeed."

Key Findings from My Research: How Organizations Can Prepare for Gen Z Leaders

As Gen Z steps into leadership roles, organizations must rethink traditional leadership development and build structures that align with how this generation thinks, works, and leads. My research across multiple industries—including technology, hospitality, education, and manufacturing—reveals key trends that companies must act on now to remain competitive in the evolving workplace.

The following insights highlight how organizations can proactively develop Gen Z leaders and create a leadership pipeline that ensures long-term success.

Develop Leadership Pathways That Include Both People Leadership and Expert Leadership

Not all high-performing employees want to manage people—but that doesn't mean they lack leadership potential. Gen Z values leadership based on expertise, collaboration, and influence rather than just job titles or years of experience.

Many organizations still follow a traditional promotion structure, where leadership means moving into a managerial role. But for Gen Z, leadership must be more flexible, allowing them to grow without being forced into people management.

What Organizations Should Do:

- Create dual leadership tracks—Offer career advancement options that allow employees to choose between traditional people management roles or leadership through expertise.
- Recognize thought leadership and project ownership—Leadership should not be measured solely by how many direct reports an employee has but also by how they contribute to innovation, problem-solving, and mentorship.
- Provide leadership development for all high-potential employees—Ensure that both people-focused and technical leaders receive training in strategy, influence, and decision making.

Key Takeaway

Leadership is no longer one-size-fits-all. Companies that offer alternative leadership pathways will retain top Gen Z talent and create a more diverse, adaptable leadership pipeline.

Train Leaders to Balance Autonomy with Structure

One of the biggest misconceptions about Gen Z is that they crave unlimited flexibility. My research shows that what they actually want is structured autonomy—clear expectations and direction, but with the trust to execute their work independently.

Traditional leadership models often fall into two extremes:

Micromanagement, where employees feel suffocated by unnecessary oversight.

Hands-off leadership, where employees feel unsupported due to vague guidance.

Neither approach works. Gen Z leaders will be most effective when they learn to strike the right balance.

What Organizations Should Do:

- Teach future leaders how to set clear goals without micromanaging. Employees thrive when they know what is expected, why it matters, and how success will be measured.
- Encourage structured check-ins. Leadership training should emphasize regular feedback loops, where employees get guidance and accountability without unnecessary oversight.
- Define decision-making boundaries. Leaders should be trained on when to step in and when to let employees take ownership of projects or challenges.

Key Takeaway

Leadership development programs must teach Gen Z how to balance autonomy and structure. When organizations get this right, employees feel empowered and engaged—without the frustration of unclear expectations or overbearing management.

Create Transparent Decision-Making Structures

Gen Z values fairness, equity, and transparency—especially when it comes to how leadership decisions are made. My research confirms that organizations that operate behind closed doors breed distrust and disengagement.

Unlike past generations, who may have accepted "trust the process" leadership, Gen Z expects:

Clear explanations of why promotions, raises, and leadership decisions happen.

Opportunities to give input before major company decisions are finalized.

Access to leadership discussions, rather than vague policies handed down from above.

Companies that fail to meet these expectations risk losing Gen Z leaders who feel left out of the process.

What Organizations Should Do:

- Formalize decision-making structures. Implement documented, consistent processes for performance evaluations, promotions, and strategic changes.
- Encourage collaborative leadership. Train leaders to seek input from employees before making major decisions—this builds trust and strengthens engagement.
- Make leadership accessible. Host open forums, town halls, or Q&A sessions where employees can ask leadership direct questions about company direction and decision making.

Key Takeaway

Transparency isn't just about making employees feel included—it directly impacts retention and engagement. Companies that actively involve employees in decision making will build stronger, more loyal teams and prevent frustration-driven turnover.

Invest in Continuous Leadership Development

Historically, leadership development was reserved for executives and senior managers. Employees were expected to "work their way up" before they received formal leadership training.

That approach is outdated.

Gen Z expects leadership training to begin early, long before they step into formal management roles. Organizations that wait until employees reach midcareer stages will lose top talent to competitors that invest in early leadership development.

What Organizations Should Do:

- Start leadership training early. Offer mentorship programs, stretch assignments, and coaching to identify and nurture future leaders from entry-level positions.
- Make leadership training an ongoing process. Instead of one-time workshops, provide continuous learning opportunities through online courses, leadership academies, and peer coaching.
- Ensure leadership training includes emotional intelligence, adaptability, and digital fluency. The best leaders of the future will need a mix of interpersonal skills, tech-savviness, and strategic thinking.

Key Takeaway

Leadership isn't a one-time milestone—it's a continuous journey. Organizations that integrate leadership development at every career stage will retain top talent and future-proof their workforce.

Final Thought: The Future of Leadership Starts Now

Gen Z isn't the future of leadership—they are already leading. Organizations that embrace this shift, invest in leadership development, and adapt their structures will thrive.

Companies that fail to evolve will struggle with higher turnover, disengagement, and outdated leadership models that no longer resonate with today's workforce.

The choice is simple: Prepare for the next generation of leaders now, or risk losing them to organizations that do.

The Next Challenge: Preparing for Generation Alpha (2013–2025)

While Gen Alpha is still entering the education system, they are already being shaped by a radically different world than any generation before them. This generation will enter the workforce fully immersed in AI, automation, and digital-first communication, with unprecedented access to information, learning tools, and career paths that didn't exist for previous generations. Unlike Gen Z, who grew up adapting to technological advancements, Gen Alpha has never known a world without them.

For leaders, this presents a critical challenge and opportunity. Organizations that wait too long to adapt will find themselves struggling to retain top talent, while forward-thinking leaders who prepare now will be the ones who shape the future workplace.

How Gen Alpha Will Redefine Leadership Expectations

Every generation has redefined the workplace in its own way. Baby boomers valued loyalty and hierarchy. Gen X introduced work–life balance and independence. Millennials emphasized purpose-driven work and flexibility. Gen Z has pushed for transparency, fairness, and engagement.

Gen Alpha? They will expect a leadership model that is digital-first, highly adaptable, and deeply personalized.

The best leaders will start preparing now by addressing three key shifts.

Leadership Development Will Need to Start Earlier

In previous generations, leadership development was something employees "earned" over time. Employees worked their way up through the ranks, often reaching leadership roles only in their 30s, 40s, or beyond.

That model is already shifting. Gen Z has accelerated the demand for early leadership opportunities, and Gen Alpha will push it even further.

By the time they enter the workforce, Gen Alpha will have spent years using AI-powered learning platforms, self-directed career development tools, and digital mentorship programs that allow them to acquire leadership skills faster than any previous generation.

This means:

- Waiting until midcareer to invest in leadership training will be too late. Companies will need to spot leadership potential early and provide structured development paths much sooner than before.
- Traditional career ladders will need to be replaced with career lattices. Gen Alpha won't want to wait in line for a promotion

based on tenure alone. They will expect horizontal movement, cross-functional leadership opportunities, and skill-based promotions.

- Leadership training won't just be for managers—it will be for everyone. The companies that succeed will be those that embed leadership training at every level, ensuring employees are prepared to lead long before they have a formal title.

Key Takeaway

Start building leadership skills earlier. If organizations fail to do this, they'll lose top talent to companies that invest in early leadership development.

Adaptability and Digital Fluency Will Be Nonnegotiable

Gen Alpha will be the most technologically fluent workforce in history. AI, automation, and digital tools won't be optional enhancements—they will be the foundation of how work gets done.

For leaders, this means staying ahead of the curve in digital transformation, or risk being outpaced by their own employees.

- Leaders will need to utilize AI, not fear it. While some organizations still hesitate to integrate AI into their workflows, Gen Alpha will expect AI to be an essential tool for decision making, efficiency, and innovation. Leaders who resist technology will lose credibility.
- Data-driven leadership will be the standard. Gen Alpha will question gut-based decisions and expect leadership to justify decisions with clear, transparent data. Organizations that fail to integrate data into their leadership strategy will be seen as outdated and untrustworthy.
- Digital communication will replace traditional management styles. Leaders will need to excel in remote collaboration, asynchronous decision making, and AI-enhanced communication. The old model of "leading by presence" will be irrelevant—leaders will be expected to manage teams effectively, regardless of physical location.

Key Takeaway

Leadership will no longer be about "who's been around the longest" or "who knows the right people." It will be about who can adapt quickly, leverage technology, and lead effectively in a digital-first world.

Traditional Workplace Structures Will Become Obsolete

The concept of a 9-to-5, office-based job is already fading, and by the time Gen Alpha enters the workforce, it will likely be a relic of the past.

For this generation, remote and hybrid work won't be a temporary solution—it will be the norm. They will have grown up watching their parents and older siblings work from home, collaborate across time zones, and leverage technology to replace in-person meetings.

This means leadership will need to evolve beyond the traditional, location-based model.

- Decentralized leadership will be critical. Leadership will no longer be limited to those in corporate offices. Companies will need to develop leaders across remote teams, regional hubs, and digital-first workplaces.
- Flexibility will be a competitive advantage. While some organizations still cling to rigid work schedules, Gen Alpha will choose employers that offer autonomy and adaptability. Companies that force outdated workplace structures will struggle to attract and retain talent.
- Work–life integration will replace work–life balance. For Gen Alpha, work and personal life won't be separate spheres—they will expect seamless integration, allowing them to work when and how they are most productive. Leaders will need to shift from enforcing hours worked to measuring results achieved.

Key Takeaway

Companies that fail to accept hybrid and remote-friendly leadership models will find themselves unable to attract top Gen Alpha talent.

Preparing for the Future: What Leaders Must Do Now

Leadership is already evolving, but the pace of change is about to accelerate. Waiting until Gen Alpha enters the workforce to adapt will be too late.

To stay ahead, organizations should:

1. Redesign leadership pipelines to start earlier. Identify and nurture leadership potential before employees reach midcareer.
2. Train leaders to be tech-forward. Ensure managers are AI literate, data driven, and comfortable leading in digital-first environments.
3. Dismantle outdated workplace structures. Embrace flexibility, remote leadership, and decentralized decision making.

Gen Alpha won't settle for workplaces that feel outdated, inefficient, or slow to adapt. They will choose leaders and organizations that accept and implement change, empower employees, and leverage technology to build a better way of working.

The best leaders aren't waiting for the future to arrive. They are shaping it now.

Final Thought: The Organizations That Adapt Will Win

The future of leadership is not about eliminating structure—it's about creating leadership models that are transparent, empowering, and adaptable. My research shows that Gen Z is not rejecting leadership, but redefining it to be more collaborative, expertise driven, and focused on enabling teams to succeed.

This shift is not happening in isolation. For the first time in modern history, organizations must navigate a workforce with five active generations—from baby boomers delaying retirement to Gen Alpha entering the early stages of employment within the next decade. This creates a unique challenge and opportunity for leadership models:

- Gen Z leaders will be tasked with managing a workforce that is more generationally diverse than any before. Unlike previous generations, who primarily worked alongside two or three co-horts, Gen Z leaders must bridge the communication and leadership gap between boomers, Gen X, millennials, their own Gen Z peers, and eventually, Gen Alpha.

- Retirement is shifting. My research suggests that people are retiring later due to economic factors and increased longevity, meaning that Gen Z will likely manage professionals with decades more experience than themselves.
- Gen Alpha's leadership expectations are still forming, but early indicators suggest they will have even greater expectations for digital fluency, real-time feedback, and flexible work environments. They are growing up in a world where AI and automation are the norm, which will reshape the way leadership functions.

Organizations that understand this complexity and proactively evolve their leadership models will win. The companies that remain rigid—clinging to outdated, hierarchical, and closed-door leadership models—will struggle to attract and retain talent across multiple generations.

Preparing for the Future: The Companies That Lead Will Lead

Businesses that embrace the evolution of leadership today will set the standard for the workforce of the future. This means:

- Creating adaptable leadership structures that allow for both expertise-based and people-based leadership pathways.
- Investing in generational intelligence—training leaders to understand and engage multiple generations effectively.
- Embedding continuous learning into leadership development, ensuring managers are equipped to handle shifting workforce expectations.
- Utilizing technology not as a replacement for leadership, but as a tool to enhance transparency, structure, and engagement.

Companies that recognize and prepare for these shifts will not just survive the future of leadership—they will define it. The next decade will belong to organizations that embody transparency, empower their teams, and create environments where the next generation of leaders thrives.

Key Takeaways from Part 4: The Future of Leadership and The Rise of Gen Z Leaders

Leadership is undergoing a fundamental transformation, and the Engaged Empathy Leadership Model (EELM) provides the framework for this shift. As workforce expectations evolve, technology advances, and organizational structures become more fluid, leaders must adapt or risk falling behind.

Gen Z is already redefining leadership by prioritizing collaboration, transparency, and expertise-driven influence over traditional top-down authority. Organizations that embrace this shift will thrive, while those that cling to outdated leadership models will struggle to attract and retain talent.

The Future of Engaged Empathy Leadership Model (EELM)

EELM is not a static leadership model—it is designed to evolve as workplaces continue to change. The core pillars of kindness, fairness, and structure will remain, but how they are implemented will continue to be refined as new challenges emerge.

- Kindness will become a companywide strategy, not just an individual leadership trait. Emotional intelligence, psychological safety, and employee well-being initiatives will be embedded into organizational culture and leadership training.
- Fairness will be driven by data and transparency. AI and people analytics will play a larger role in detecting bias in hiring, promotions, and pay decisions, ensuring leadership decisions are backed by objective, measurable criteria.
- Structure will evolve to balance flexibility with accountability. Companies will adopt hybrid leadership structures that blend traditional decision making with decentralized, team-driven leadership, creating an environment where employees feel both empowered and supported.

Key Takeaway

Leaders who implement EELM effectively will create work environments that foster long-term trust, engagement, and retention—ensuring that leadership is not just reactive but forward-thinking.

The Rise of Gen Z as Leaders

Gen Z isn't just changing the workplace—they're stepping into leadership roles at an unprecedented pace. Unlike previous generations, their approach to leadership is less about authority and more about expertise, influence, and collaboration.

- Leadership is shifting from authority to influence. Employees no longer respect leadership based on titles alone—they follow leaders who demonstrate competence, fairness, and an ability to engage.
- A dual-track leadership model will emerge:
  - People Leaders—Those who focus on team development, coaching, and traditional management.
  - Expert Leaders—Individual contributors who lead through technical skill, project management, and innovation—without necessarily managing teams.
- Leadership will move away from micromanagement and toward empowerment. Gen Z leaders will focus on enabling teams, removing obstacles, and setting clear expectations, rather than dictating every step of the process.

Key Takeaway

Organizations that recognize and develop these two leadership tracks will retain and empower high-potential employees—ensuring that leadership fits modern workforce needs rather than forcing outdated management styles.

Preparing for a Multigenerational Workforce

For the first time in history, workplaces will have five generations working side by side. Gen Z leaders will be responsible for managing teams that include baby boomers, Gen X, millennials, fellow Gen Z employees, and soon, Gen Alpha.

- Retirement trends are shifting. Many baby boomers and Gen X professionals are delaying retirement, meaning Gen Z leaders will need to manage employees with significantly more experience than them.
- Generational leadership styles will clash. Older generations may expect traditional authority structures, while younger employees will prefer decentralized, team-based leadership.
- Gen Alpha's leadership expectations are already forming. They will demand even greater transparency, digital fluency, and flexibility in leadership—organizations must begin preparing now for what's coming.

Key Takeaway

Companies that invest in leadership training now—focusing on multi-generational leadership, communication, and adaptability—will position themselves as the best places to work for employees of all generations.

The Organizations That Adapt Will Win

The companies that embrace this leadership shift today will define the workforce of the future.

- The most successful companies will prioritize adaptable leadership structures. Rigid, hierarchical leadership will give way to transparent, flexible, and expertise-driven models.
- Technology should enhance, not replace, leadership. AI and automation must be used to support leadership development, improve communication, and track fairness metrics—but leadership itself must remain human-centered.
- Continuous learning will be essential. Leadership development will no longer be a one-time event—it must be ongoing, structured, and designed to evolve with workforce expectations.

Key Takeaway

Businesses that commit to modernizing leadership now will attract, retain, and develop the next generation of high-performing talent—while those that resist will struggle to stay competitive.

Final Thought: Leadership Must Evolve

Workplaces will keep changing, and leadership has to change right along with them.

The best leaders don't dig their heels in and pine for the "good old days." They adapt, learn, and evolve—not just for themselves but for the people they lead. Because leadership isn't about holding onto the past— it's about building a future people *want* to be part of.

Engaged Empathy Leadership Model (EELM) isn't some feel-good trend—it's the blueprint for what leadership needs to be. It's not a choice between driving results or building relationships—it's about knowing how to do both and doing them well.

The leaders and companies that embrace this shift won't just keep up—they'll set the pace. The ones who don't? Well, they'll be looking around wondering where everybody went.

Bonus Chapters

The Toolbox: Applying the Engaged Empathy Leadership Model

The Toolbox: Turning Engaged Empathy Leadership Model into Action

Leadership isn't just about understanding concepts—it's about putting them into action. Throughout this book, you've explored the key pillars of the Engaged Empathy Leadership Model (EELM) and how they shape effective leadership in today's workplaces. Now, it's time to apply them.

The Toolbox serves as a bridge between theory and practice, offering structured, adaptable exercises that reinforce fairness, kindness, and structure in real workplace situations. These tools are designed to help leaders, educators, and employees move beyond abstract ideas and create tangible, lasting impact within their teams and organizations.

What's Inside the Toolbox?

- All exercises from the book—A quick-reference guide so you can find and use them without flipping back through chapters.
- Additional exercises and variations—New ways to apply fairness, kindness, and structure across different workplace settings.
- Prompts for reflection and discussion—Thought-provoking questions to deepen your understanding and encourage real-world application.

Using the Toolbox for Continuous Improvement

Leadership development isn't a one-time effort—it's an ongoing process. The exercises in this section are designed not just for single-use scenarios but for continuous learning and improvement over time. Here's how you can use them to foster long-term growth:

- Repeat and Reassess: Many exercises can be revisited periodically to track progress, identify changes in leadership effectiveness, and refine strategies over time.
- Encourage Peer Learning: Use these exercises in team meetings, leadership workshops, or training sessions to foster collaboration and shared learning.
- Gather Feedback and Adapt: After completing an exercise, gather feedback from participants to refine the approach and customize it for your workplace's unique needs.
- Integrate into Organizational Culture: These exercises aren't just one-off activities—they can shape how leadership, communication, and decision making evolve within an organization.

How to Get the Most Out of the Exercises

- Try them solo—Use them for personal leadership development to refine your self-awareness and decision making.
- Facilitate group discussions—Apply them in workshops, classrooms, or team meetings to encourage open dialogue and strengthen team culture.
- Adapt them to your organization—Whether you're in a small business, corporate setting, or educational environment, these exercises can be tailored to fit your team's needs.

Pro Tip: Try these exercises with your team or colleagues to build trust, encourage open discussions, and develop a stronger, more engaged workplace culture. Leadership is a journey, not a destination, and these tools will help you continuously grow, adapt, and lead with engaged empathy.

Empathy-Building Exercise for Managers: "Know Your Team"

The "Know Your Team" initiative is a structured, yet flexible leadership exercise designed to help managers build meaningful relationships with their teams without crossing professional boundaries. This program encourages leaders to understand their employees beyond just job roles and performance metrics.

Step 1—Gathering Insight—Employee Connection Profiles:

- Each employee fills out a brief, voluntary questionnaire with both professional and fun connection questions.

Required Questions (Work-Centered):

- What motivates you at work?
- What's one thing you appreciate in a great manager?
- What's a small workplace gesture that makes your day better?
- Do you prefer structured check-ins or more casual interactions?
- Coffee, tea, or neither? Favorite snack?

Optional Fun Connection Questions (For Managers Who Want to Add Personality to Check-Ins):

- What's your favorite movie that came out in the 1980s?
- What's the worst month of the year and why?
- If you could pick one theme song that plays every time you enter a meeting, what would it be?
- What's your ultimate guilty pleasure snack?
- What's a minor inconvenience that irrationally annoys you?

These fun questions add personality to workplace relationships without crossing professional boundaries. Managers can opt to use them when appropriate—some employees may love answering them, while others may prefer to stick to work-related topics.

Step 2—Using Fun Questions to Build Organic Connection:

- For informal team meetings—Rotate one fun question at the start of weekly check-ins to lighten the mood and encourage casual conversation.

- For one-on-one check-ins—If an employee mentions loving Reese's Cups, surprising them with one after a tough week is a small gesture that shows thoughtfulness.
- For new employees—Including a mix of work and personal questions in onboarding forms helps managers remember small details that make engagement more natural over time.

Example:

A manager notices that an employee listed "August" as their least favorite month because they hate the heat. When August rolls around, the manager jokes about surviving the worst month together or suggests an iced coffee run to beat the heat. These small, thoughtful moments create genuine connections.

Thought—Adding Personality Without Forcing It:

- Let employees choose what level of engagement feels right for them—some will love these quirky questions, while others may prefer to keep things work-focused.
- Use these insights naturally. A leader who casually references someone's favorite candy or worst month in a lighthearted way demonstrates kindness without being intrusive.
- Keep it fun, not forced. The goal is to create organic interactions, not to turn leadership into a social club.

Step 3—Encouraging Peer-to-Peer Connection:

- Managers model teamwide kindness by encouraging employees to participate in structured but low-pressure team engagement.
- Some ideas:
  - "Appreciation Rounds" where employees highlight a teammate's contribution during weekly meetings.
  - "Reverse Mentorship" programs where employees at different levels exchange insights on leadership, work culture, and collaboration.

○ "Team Preferences Wall" (physical or digital) where employees voluntarily list their work style preferences (e.g., "I focus best with headphones on" or "I'm always happy to brainstorm over coffee").

By embedding kindness into leadership training, organizations create a sustainable culture of respect and engagement—one where employees feel genuinely seen, not just managed.

Virtual Version: "Know Your Team" Exercise

In today's workplaces, connection-building is just as important in virtual and hybrid environments as it is in physical offices. The *Virtual "Know Your Team" Initiative* ensures that managers and employees can build meaningful professional relationships, regardless of location.

Step 1—Gathering Insights—Digital Employee Connection Profiles:

Managers can set up a *Google Form, Microsoft Teams survey, or Slack poll* where employees answer both professional and fun connection questions.

Required Questions (Work Centered):

- What motivates you at work?
- What's one thing you appreciate in a great manager?
- What's a small workplace gesture that makes your day better?
- Do you prefer structured check-ins or more casual interactions?
- How do you like to receive recognition for your work?

Optional Fun Connection Questions (For Managers Who Want to Add Personality to Check-Ins):

- What's your favorite movie that came out in the 1980s?
- What's the worst month of the year and why?
- If you could pick one theme song that plays every time you enter a meeting, what would it be?

- What's your ultimate guilty pleasure snack?
- What's a minor inconvenience that irrationally annoys you?

These fun questions add personality to workplace relationships without crossing professional boundaries. Managers can opt to use them when appropriate—some employees may enjoy answering them, while others may prefer to stick to work-related topics.

Step 2—Using Virtual Interactions to Build Connection:

- **Start virtual meetings with a fun question**—Use Zoom polls, chat responses, or quick Slack threads to lighten the mood.
- **Digital check-ins**—If an employee mentions a favorite coffee or snack, send them a **digital gift card** after a tough project to show appreciation.
- **Recognition in team e-mails or chats**—Use a dedicated Slack or Teams channel for employee recognition where team members can highlight contributions.

Example: A manager notices that an employee mentioned they work best in the morning and prefer fewer afternoon meetings. When scheduling a project check-in, the manager intentionally sets it for the morning instead of the afternoon and casually acknowledges, "I know you're at your best earlier in the day, so I figured we'd catch up now." This small, thoughtful adjustment shows that the manager values their preferences, reinforcing a culture of respect and engagement.

Step 3—Encouraging Virtual Peer-to-Peer Kindness:

- Reverse Mentorship via Virtual Coffee Chats—Pair employees across levels for casual 15-minute video chats to exchange insights on leadership, work culture, and collaboration.
- **Virtual "Team Preferences" Board**—Use a shared Google Doc, Miro board, or Slack thread where employees can voluntarily list their work styles (e.g., "I focus best with Slack notifications off" or "I'm always happy to brainstorm over a quick call").

- **Appreciation Rounds**—During teamwide video meetings, employees take a moment to highlight a colleague's contribution to reinforce positive workplace culture.

By embedding kindness into leadership training, organizations create a sustainable culture of respect and engagement—one where employees feel genuinely seen, not just managed. This virtual-friendly version ensures that relationship-building is not limited to in-person teams.

Kindness in Action: The "Micro-Moments of Leadership" Challenge

A Simple Yet Powerful Way to Embed Kindness in Everyday Workplace Culture

Objective:

- Help leaders and employees recognize that small, intentional acts of kindness can have a major impact on workplace morale.
- Shift kindness from being occasional or performative to being an embedded, everyday leadership habit.
- Encourage employees at all levels to contribute to a culture of kindness.

How It Works:

For 1 week, participants intentionally practice at least one "micro-moment" of kindness per day—small, low-effort actions that strengthen relationships and morale.

Step 1—Framing the Challenge (Kickoff Discussion— 15 Minutes):

- Discuss the impact of kindness in leadership: How does thoughtfulness and generosity influence team culture and engagement?
- Challenge participants to notice and record small moments of kindness they experience or initiate throughout the week.

Step 2—The Micro-Moment Challenge
(1 Week, Self-Directed):

Each day, participants choose one small, intentional act of kindness in the workplace.
Examples of Micro-Moments:

- Acknowledging unseen work: Publicly recognize a teammate for behind-the-scenes contributions.
- Thoughtful follow-up: If a colleague mentioned a stressful project, ask how it's going later in the week.
- Small surprises: Send a short thank-you message, forward an article of interest, or bring an extra coffee for someone.
- Creating space: In a meeting, invite someone who hasn't spoken much to share their thoughts.
- Expressing care: If someone seems off, check in: "Hey, I noticed you've been quiet today. Everything OK?"

Step 3—The Reflection Wrap-Up (Team Discussion—
20 Minutes):

At the end of the week, the team briefly discusses:

- What micro-moments stood out to you?
- Did you notice a change in how you felt or how others responded?
- How can we make these acts of kindness a regular part of our workplace culture?

Why This Works:

- Removes pressure—kindness doesn't need to be grand or time-consuming.
- Demonstrates impact—small actions accumulate into meaningful workplace culture shifts.
- Encourages consistency—helps kindness become an embedded behavior, not just a one-time initiative.

This exercise is a low-lift, high-impact way to make kindness a daily leadership habit, ensuring it translates into real workplace behaviors, not just an abstract value.

The Ripple Effect of Kindness: A Workplace Kindness Workshop

A Scalable Workshop for Small and Large Organizations

Objective:

- Help employees and leaders experience firsthand the impact of kindness in the workplace.
- Encourage cross-departmental connection and engagement.
- Shift kindness from being an individual practice to an organizational culture driver.

How It Works:

This interactive workshop guides participants through an experiential exercise where they witness how kindness spreads across an organization, demonstrating its compounding effects on morale, engagement, and trust.

Step 1—Framing the Concept (10 Minutes):

- The facilitator introduces the concept of "The Ripple Effect"— the idea that one small act of kindness can set off a chain reaction of positive workplace interactions.
- The group discusses:
  - Have you ever received a small act of kindness at work that made a difference in your day?
  - How does kindness impact engagement, productivity, and retention?
  - What holds people back from expressing kindness in a professional setting?

Step 2—The Ripple Effect Experiment (30 Minutes):

This interactive exercise demonstrates how kindness spreads through a workplace. It works in both small and large organizations and can be conducted in-person or virtually.

Instructions:

- Each participant is given a "kindness action card" with a small action they must complete during the session.
- The actions are designed to be simple but meaningful, such as:
  - "Thank someone specifically for their hard work this week."
  - "Send a quick note of encouragement to a colleague."
  - "Recognize someone outside of your department."
  - "Ask a colleague how they're doing and truly listen."
  - "Share something positive about a team project."
- After a few minutes of completing their action, the facilitator asks:
  - How did it feel to give or receive kindness?
  - Did anyone experience a kindness ripple—where one action led to another?

Large Organizations Variation:

- Instead of individual kindness actions, groups of 5 to 10 employees work together on a kindness chain reaction.
- Example: The first person recognizes a teammate, the teammate passes along gratitude, and so on.
- This version helps show how kindness can travel across teams and departments in a large-scale setting.

Step 3—The Reflection and Workplace Application (20 Minutes):

- Participants reflect on how kindness isn't just "nice" but a strategic tool for engagement and collaboration.
- Small and large groups discuss:
  - What small kindness actions resonated most?
  - How can we encourage kindness in our team culture?
  - What barriers prevent kindness in the workplace, and how can we overcome them?
- Commitment Challenge: Each participant writes down one small but consistent kindness habit they will practice moving forward.

Why This Works:

- Scalable for any organization—can be done with small teams or across departments.
- Interactive and memorable—experiencing kindness creates stronger engagement than just discussing it.
- Builds a sustainable kindness culture—participants leave with real, repeatable actions.

Follow-Up Idea:

Organizations can create a "Kindness Board" (physical or digital) where employees share small kindness actions they witness in real time. This keeps the ripple effect going long after the workshop ends.

Kindness in Crisis: A Leadership Reflection and Application Exercise

A Practical Activity for Building Compassionate Leadership in High-Pressure Situations

Objective:

- Help leaders and employees recognize how kindness plays a role in navigating workplace challenges.
- Encourage leaders to reflect on how they respond under pressure and identify ways to integrate kindness into crisis management.
- Provide teams with a practical framework to ensure kindness is not overlooked during stressful situations.

Step 1—Individual Reflection (10 Minutes):

Each participant reflects on and writes about a time when a leader's kindness made a difference during a high-stakes or difficult situation.
Reflection Prompts:

- Think of a time when you or your team faced a major challenge, setback, or crisis at work.

- Did a leader or colleague show kindness in a way that changed the experience for you?
- What specific action or words made the difference?
- How did it impact the outcome, morale, or long-term trust in the leader?
- If kindness was missing, how might the situation have been different if a leader had responded with more empathy?

Participants write a brief summary of their experience, focusing on what was learned from it.

Step 2—Small Group Discussion (15–20 Minutes, Optional for Large Groups):

- Participants break into small groups of three to five people to share their reflections.
- Each person briefly explains:
  - The situation
  - The act (or absence) of kindness
  - How it influenced the outcome
- Group members discuss:
  - Are there patterns in how kindness showed up in different crises?
  - What types of leadership behaviors made the biggest difference?
  - How can we ensure kindness is a leadership priority, even under stress?

Step 3—Crisis Kindness Framework (15 Minutes):

Now that participants have explored past experiences, they shift to building a framework for applying kindness in future crises.

Introducing the Three-Part Crisis Kindness Model:

1. Pause and Assess—Before reacting, take a moment to recognize the emotional and practical needs of the team.
   - Ask: "What do people need from me right now—reassurance, clarity, action?"

2. Communicate with Empathy—Even in tough conversations, tone and delivery matter.
   ○ Instead of "We need to push harder," try "I know this is tough, and I appreciate everyone's effort. Let's tackle it together."
3. Follow Through—The greatest kindness in a crisis is showing up consistently.
   ○ Ensure that employees feel supported, not just during the crisis but in the aftermath.

Step 4—Leadership Application Exercise (10 Minutes):

- Each participant chooses a realistic crisis scenario from their own workplace.
- They then outline how they would apply the Crisis Kindness Model in that situation.

Examples of Workplace Crises:

- A companywide restructuring, leading to layoffs.
- A major client unexpectedly cancels a contract.
- A project deadline moves up significantly, putting pressure on employees.
- A team member makes a costly mistake that impacts operations.

Application Prompts:

- How would you pause and assess the situation before reacting?
- What is one way you could communicate with empathy while still being direct?
- What actions could you take to show follow-through and support after the crisis?

Participants share their plans with a partner or group, getting feedback on how to strengthen their leadership approach.

Why This Works:

- Encourages self-awareness—Helps leaders recognize their own crisis-response tendencies.
- Promotes practical kindness—Kindness is not just a "soft skill" but a leadership competency during challenges.
- Teaches actionable techniques—Gives leaders a framework to apply kindness in real time, even under pressure.

The Fairness Audit: Seeing Through Different Lenses

A Leadership and Employee Engagement Exercise

Fairness is not just a policy—it's a perception. A company may believe it has fair promotion, compensation, and decision-making policies, but if employees do not perceive them as fair, those policies are failing in practice.

This Fairness Audit is a structured exercise designed to help leadership teams assess fairness through the eyes of their employees. By combining self-reflection, employee feedback, and structured action planning, organizations can uncover gaps in communication and execution—ensuring that fairness is not just an intention but a reality.

Objective:

- Evaluate whether employees perceive key workplace policies (promotions, pay, career growth, and decision making) as fair
- Identify hidden gaps in communication, transparency, or execution
- Develop concrete actions to improve fairness in workplace policies

Step 1—Leadership Fairness Reflection (Pre-Exercise Homework—15 Minutes):

Before engaging with employee feedback, leaders complete a self-assessment on fairness in the workplace. This step forces leadership to examine their own assumptions without being influenced by immediate data.

Instructions:

- Each leader and HR team member completes the self-assessment individually before reviewing employee responses.
- Responses should be honest and reflective.

Reflection Questions for Leadership:

- On a scale of 1 to 5, how fair do you believe our company's promotion process is?
- Are employees fully aware of what is required to advance? How do we ensure they know?
- Do we clearly communicate how pay raises and bonuses are determined?
- What do we think employees would say is the biggest obstacle to career growth here?
- When was the last time a tough decision (promotion, reorganization, pay policy) was explained clearly to employees?

Why It Matters:

- Establishes a baseline perception from leadership before seeing employee feedback
- Helps identify potential blind spots in fairness perceptions
- Prepares leaders for a data-driven discussion in later steps

Step 2—Employee Fairness Perception Survey (Anonymous—15 Minutes):

After leadership completes their self-assessment, employees provide their actual experiences through an anonymous survey. This allows organizations to compare leadership's expectations with employee realities.

Survey Format:

- Mix of 1 to 5 scale ratings and open-ended responses
- Can be conducted via Google Forms, Microsoft Teams, or an internal company survey tool

Sample Survey Questions:

- I understand what is required to advance in my career at this company (1–5 scale)
- The promotion process here feels transparent and fair (1–5 scale)
- When I receive a raise, I understand how the decision was made (1–5 scale)
- I feel comfortable asking leadership about career growth opportunities (1–5 scale)
- What's one thing we could do to improve fairness in promotions or pay? (open-ended)

Why It Matters:

- Captures real-time, anonymous data on fairness perceptions
- Helps leadership identify misalignment between policies and employee experiences
- Highlights areas where communication or execution needs improvement

Step 3—The Fairness Blind Spot Challenge
(Group Discussion—30 Minutes):

Leaders and HR teams review the self-assessments and compare them with employee survey data. The goal is to identify the biggest gaps in perception.

Discussion Prompts:

- What surprised you? Did leadership rate fairness higher than employees did?
- Where are the biggest gaps? If employees overwhelmingly say they don't understand the promotion process, but leadership assumes they do, this highlights a communication issue.
- What policies need more transparency? If employees feel raises are inconsistent, does the company need clearer salary banding or better communication about pay decisions?
- Do employees feel comfortable advocating for themselves? If not, what structural barriers might be preventing that?

Example Discussion Outcome:

- Leadership's assumption: "Employees understand our promotion process because it's outlined in the handbook."
- Employee reality: "We don't know how promotions work because the handbook is vague, and no one explains the process clearly."
- Action needed: Develop a transparent promotion roadmap that is actively communicated, not just written in a document.

Step 4—Fairness Action Plan (Commitment to Change— 15 Minutes):

This exercise is not just about awareness—it's about making fairness actionable.

Leaders commit to at least one tangible action that will improve fairness and transparency in promotions, pay, or decision making.

Examples of Actionable Changes:

- Hosting quarterly "Ask Me Anything" (AMA) sessions where employees can ask leadership about promotions and pay
- Making salary bands and advancement requirements public
- Reworking performance review templates to clarify how employees are evaluated
- Providing employees with structured career growth roadmaps

Each leadership team selects one action that can be implemented within the next 30 to 60 days.

Why This Works:

- Forces leaders to confront fairness blind spots through real employee data
- Engages employees in the fairness conversation without making it feel like an abstract HR issue
- Results in concrete policy changes rather than just another "listening session"

Use This Exercise as a Recurring Leadership Practice:

To ensure fairness is a continuous priority, organizations can conduct this Fairness Audit annually and track progress based on employee feedback.

Fairness in Action: The Decision-Making Transparency Exercise

A Leadership Activity to Strengthen Trust and Fairness in Workplace Decisions

Many workplace fairness issues stem from a lack of transparency in decision making. Employees may not feel that promotions, workload distribution, or policy changes are fair—not necessarily because they disagree with the decisions, but because they don't understand how those decisions were made.

This exercise helps leadership teams examine how transparent their decision-making processes are and identify opportunities to increase fairness through better communication, inclusivity, and clarity.

Objective:

- Assess how workplace decisions (promotions, pay, restructuring, work assignments, etc.) are communicated and whether employees perceive them as fair.
- Improve leadership transparency by ensuring employees understand who makes decisions, how they are made, and why.
- Strengthen employee trust and engagement by making fairness an ongoing priority in workplace policies.

Step 1—Decision-Making Transparency Self-assessment (15 Minutes):

Leaders complete a self-assessment on how major workplace decisions are made and communicated.

Instructions:

Each leadership team member reflects individually before discussing responses as a group.

Self-Assessment Questions:

- Who is involved in major decisions about promotions, pay, or job assignments?
- How often do employees receive clear explanations about these decisions?
- Do employees feel they have a voice in decisions that impact them?
- Have we ever been surprised by employee backlash to a decision we thought was fair?
- How do we communicate why a decision was made, not just what the decision is?

Step 2—The Decision Transparency Gap Analysis (30 Minutes):

Leadership team discussion comparing self-assessment responses.
Discussion Prompts:

- Where are the biggest transparency gaps?
- Do we assume employees understand a decision when we haven't actually explained it?
- How do we handle tough decisions (e.g., promotions, layoffs, salary changes)?
- Do employees have opportunities to ask questions about decisions before they go into effect?
- Would employees say our decision-making process is consistent and predictable or unclear and arbitrary?

Example Discussion Outcome:

- Leadership's assumption: "We announce all promotions in a teamwide e-mail, so everyone knows how decisions are made."
- Employee reality: "We don't understand what goes into promotions. The decisions feel like a black box."
- Action needed: Develop a more transparent promotion roadmap and allow employees to ask follow-up questions in a quarterly town hall.

Step 3—The Leadership Transparency Commitment (20 Minutes):

Leaders identify one small but meaningful change they can implement immediately to increase fairness in workplace decision making.

Examples of Actionable Changes:

- Creating a simple "How We Make Decisions" document outlining key workplace policies.
- Holding quarterly leadership Q&A sessions where employees can ask about decisions that impact them.
- Training managers to provide clear explanations for promotions, pay changes, and performance evaluations.
- Introducing a decision preview step—when leadership is about to roll out a major change, they first gather employee feedback before finalizing it.

Why This Works:

- Helps leadership uncover blind spots in decision-making fairness.
- Ensures employees feel informed, heard, and valued.
- Builds organizational trust by making decision making more transparent.
- Shifts workplace culture from "just accept the decision" to "here's how and why we made this decision."

Use This Exercise to Strengthen Fairness Culture:

Conduct this Decision Transparency Audit every 6 to 12 months to ensure fairness remains a leadership priority. A fair workplace isn't just about making good decisions—it's about making those decisions clear and understandable to everyone involved.

The Fairness Check-In: A 5-Minute Leadership Habit

An Ongoing, Low-Effort Exercise to Keep Fairness at the Forefront

Objective:

- Encourage leaders to routinely reflect on fairness in their decisions.
- Create a habit of proactive fairness awareness instead of only addressing it when issues arise.
- Ensure employees feel seen, valued, and included in everyday workplace interactions.

How It Works:

At the end of each week, leaders take 5 minutes to reflect on fairness in their workplace decisions using three quick prompts.

Step 1—Weekly Fairness Reflection (5 Minutes):

Leaders ask themselves:

1. Who got an opportunity this week—and who didn't?
2. Did I make a decision that impacted someone's career, workload, or compensation? If so, did I explain it clearly?
3. Have I checked in with someone who may feel overlooked or disengaged?

Step 2—Adjust and Act (Optional, Five More Minutes If Needed):

If the reflection reveals a fairness gap, the leader takes one small action to correct it.

Examples of Small Actions:

- If someone was overlooked for an opportunity, schedule a conversation to discuss their goals and future chances.

- If a decision lacked transparency, send a quick follow-up e-mail explaining the reasoning.
- If an employee seems disengaged, take a moment to check in informally.

Why This Works:

- Makes fairness a regular leadership habit, not just a one-time event.
- Helps managers catch small fairness gaps before they become larger issues.
- Encourages self-awareness about who gets access to opportunities and recognition.
- Strengthens trust between leaders and employees through consistent, thoughtful actions.

The Decision-Making Fairness Filter

A Quick-Test Framework to Ensure Workplace Decisions Are Equitable

Objective:

- Help leaders evaluate whether a decision is fair, transparent, and consistent before implementation.
- Prevent bias and unintentional inequity in workplace policies.

How It Works:

Before making a decision, leadership teams use this four-question fairness filter:

1. Consistency Check:
   - Have we applied the same standards in similar situations?
   - Are we setting a precedent that aligns with company values?
2. Transparency Test:
   - Can we clearly explain the reasoning behind this decision to employees?
   - Have we proactively communicated key details, or will employees be caught off guard?

3. Impact Assessment:
   ○ Who benefits from this decision? Who may feel excluded or negatively impacted?
   ○ Have we considered unintended consequences, particularly for underrepresented groups?
4. Employee Voice Test:
   ○ Did we gather employee input, or are we assuming we know what's best?
   ○ Is there a way for employees to ask questions or express concerns about this decision?

Application:

- Before making compensation, promotion, or hiring decisions.
- When adjusting company policies that affect workplace culture.
- During performance evaluations to ensure fairness across teams.

Why This Works:

- Prevents leadership blind spots—Ensures leaders are not assuming fairness but actively testing it.
- Encourages accountability—Makes fairness a structured, repeatable process rather than an afterthought.
- Reduces employee distrust—When employees see a clear, consistent decision-making process, they are more likely to view it as fair.

The Leadership Transparency Framework

A Simple System to Make Decisions Clear and Understandable

Objective:

- Help leaders communicate how and why major workplace decisions are made.
- Reduce employee frustration caused by unclear promotion, compensation, or policy changes.
- Create a repeatable structure that leadership can use in all major announcements.

How It Works:

Before announcing a decision (policy change, layoffs, promotions, restructuring, etc.), leadership follows this three-step framework:

1. What's the Decision?
   ○ Clearly define what is changing.
   ○ Example: "We are adjusting how annual bonuses are calculated."
2. Why Was This Decision Made?
   ○ Explain the reasoning behind the decision.
   ○ Example: "We've found that performance-based bonuses lead to better long-term engagement."
3. How Will This Impact Employees?
   ○ Outline exactly what changes employees can expect.
   ○ Example: "Bonuses will now be tied to both individual performance and companywide metrics."

Application:

- HR and Leadership Training—Teach managers to communicate decisions effectively.
- Town Halls and All-Hands Meetings—Use this structure when rolling out new policies.
- Companywide Memos and E-mails—Ensure clear communication at every level.

Why This Works:

- Reduces misinterpretation—Employees are less likely to speculate or fill in the gaps with misinformation.
- Builds leadership credibility—Leaders who clearly communicate decisions earn trust and respect.
- Prevents unnecessary backlash—Employees don't just want to know what is changing but why.
- Ensures long-term consistency—A structured approach ensures that communication remains fair and transparent across all decisions.

The Fairness Alignment Scorecard

A Scalable Tool to Identify Where Policies and Perceptions Don't Match

Objective:

- Compare what leadership believes is fair versus what employees actually experience.
- Identify areas where policy intentions and employee perceptions do not align.
- Create measurable benchmarks for improving fairness in workplace practices.

How It Works:

Leadership and employees separately rate workplace policies using a simple 1 to 5 scale, then compare the results.

Example Scorecard Categories:

Workplace Policy	Leadership Score	Employee Score	Gap Analysis
Promotion Process Fairness	5 (Very Fair)	2 (Not Clear)	Major Gap – Needs Transparency
Pay Raise Clarity	4 (Mostly Clear)	3 (Somewhat Unclear)	Moderate Gap – Improve Communication
Decision-Making Inclusion	3 (Somewhat Fair)	1 (Not Fair)	Major Gap – Employees Feel Left Out
Career Growth Pathways	4 (Mostly Fair)	2 (Needs Clarity)	Moderate Gap – Define Promotion Criteria Better

Figure 5: The Toolbox: The Fairness Alignment Scorecard

- If leadership rates an area highly, but employees rate it low, there is a disconnect that must be addressed.
- If scores are aligned, that indicates policies are both well-structured and well-communicated.

Application:

- Use during town halls, leadership retreats, or fairness audits to track progress over time.

- Helps HR and leadership teams prioritize fairness-related improvements.
- Can be adapted for annual employee engagement surveys.

Why This Works:

- Moves fairness from assumption to data—Leadership sees real numbers instead of relying on guesswork.
- Creates measurable accountability—When fairness is quantified, it becomes easier to track progress.
- Encourages open dialogue—Employees and leadership collaborate to fix fairness gaps together.
- Can be used over time—Organizations can measure fairness annually or quarterly to track improvements.

The Role Rotation Experiment

A Hands-On Experience to Build Leadership Empathy and Improve Fairness

Objective:

- Help leaders experience the realities of frontline employees to improve decision making.
- Increase fairness by ensuring leadership fully understands the challenges of different roles before making policies.
- Reduce bias in workplace decisions by exposing leaders to multiple perspectives.

How It Works:

For 1 day, leaders shadow or participate in an entirely different role within the organization—experiencing firsthand the challenges, processes, and workflow of different teams.

Examples of Role Rotations:

- A corporate executive works a customer service shift to better understand frontline challenges.

- A senior leader sits in on an entry-level hiring process to identify where new employees struggle with onboarding.
- A department manager temporarily joins another department's team meeting to gain insight into how cross-functional collaboration works.

Debrief and Reflection:

After the rotation, participants answer:

- What surprised you about this role?
- Did this experience change how you view our current policies?
- What small changes could improve fairness and efficiency in this role?

Application:

- Works well in large and small organizations.
- Can be done as a one-time leadership retreat activity or as an ongoing initiative.
- Helps break hierarchical silos and ensures leadership decisions reflect the real challenges employees face.

Why This Works:

- Bridges the leadership–employee divide—Leaders often make decisions about roles they've never worked in; this eliminates that gap.
- Leads to policy improvements—When leaders experience challenges firsthand, they make more informed and fair decisions.
- Boosts employee trust—Employees respect leaders who understand their work, not just manage from a distance.
- Strengthens cross-department collaboration—Leaders gain insights into how teams interact and what barriers need to be addressed.

The Two-Way Town Hall: A Step-by-Step Guide for Effective Workplace Communication

A Structured Yet Engaging Approach to Leadership–Employee Dialogue

Two-way town halls are one of the most effective ways to bridge the gap between leadership and employees, particularly in today's workforce, where transparency and real-time engagement are critical. Employees, especially Gen Z, value direct access to leadership, open communication, and structured feedback mechanisms.

However, for town halls to be successful and respected, they must be structured, inclusive, and action-oriented—ensuring that all employees, whether in person or remote, feel heard. This manual provides a step-by-step framework for implementing high-impact town halls that prevent chaos, encourage meaningful dialogue, and turn employee input into real action.

Step 1: Setting the Stage—Scheduling and Accessibility:

To maximize participation, leadership must ensure that town halls are accessible to all employees, regardless of location or schedule.

- Survey employees in advance to determine the best time and frequency (quarterly, monthly, or industry-specific needs).
- Strongly encourage attendance while keeping participation voluntary. Employees should be given every opportunity to attend live.
- Offer multiple ways to attend:
  - In-Person Option: Designate a large meeting space for employees on-site.
  - Virtual Options: Provide live streaming via Zoom, Microsoft Teams, or an internal video platform.
  - Asynchronous Access: Offer a recorded version with time-stamped highlights for employees unable to join live.
- Create a standing schedule (quarterly or monthly) so employees can plan ahead and integrate it into their routines.

Step 2—Structuring the Agenda—No Free-for-Alls:

An unstructured town hall can quickly turn into a reactive, unproductive session. To ensure fairness and inclusivity, the agenda must allow for pre-planned employee participation while leaving space for real-time engagement.

- Employees submit questions in advance through an internal form, Slack thread, or e-mail.
- A public running list is displayed so employees know whose questions will be addressed, preventing interruptions and random shouting.
- Employees can still add their names during the meeting, but all contributions must follow a structured, respectful process.
- A designated facilitator (HR, senior leader, or rotating moderator) ensures discussions remain on track and every voice gets a chance to be heard.

This structure ensures that all employees, regardless of personality or seniority, have equal access to leadership.

Step 3—Facilitating the Meeting—Balancing Leadership and Employee Voices:

A successful two-way town hall balances structured discussion with interactive moments that keep employees engaged.

The moderator ensures that:

- Employees are heard without interruptions.
- Leadership actively listens rather than responding defensively.
- Key points are recorded and visible (on a whiteboard, digital screen, or shared document).

Interactive Engagement Features:

To avoid monotony and increase participation, town halls should include:

- Live Polls—Employees vote in real time on workplace topics (e.g., "Would you rather receive bonuses based on individual or team-based performance?").

- Breakout Discussions—If a major issue arises (such as a work-place policy change), small groups discuss and present insights back to leadership.
- The "Wildcard" Spot—At the start of the meeting, employees vote on a last-minute topic to be addressed at the end.

This structured flexibility ensures that the town hall remains productive and engaging while still allowing room for employee-driven discussion.

Step 4—The Closing Ritual—Management Takes a Turn:

To prevent town halls from feeling like a one-way interrogation of leadership, the session should end with leadership asking employees questions.

Leadership can pose open-ended questions such as:

- "What's one thing we're doing well that we should continue?"
- "If you could change one thing about how we communicate as a company, what would it be?"
- "What's something we aren't thinking about that we should be?"

By flipping the dynamic, leadership demonstrates a willingness to learn—not just respond.

Summarizing Key Action Items:

Before closing, leadership should briefly summarize:

- Main discussion points
- What will be followed up on
- What leadership will do next
- Expected timelines for action

Employees should leave the meeting knowing exactly how their feedback will be addressed rather than feeling like their concerns were simply acknowledged and forgotten.

Step 5—Post-Town Hall Follow-Up—Turning Words Into Action:

A town hall is only effective if employees see real follow-through on their input.

Within 48 hours, leadership should send out a recap that includes:

- Key discussion points and decisions made.
- Next steps and timelines for follow-ups.
- Any topics that require additional review and when employees can expect updates.
- Recognition of employees who contributed thoughtful feedback (without singling out negative comments).

A post-town hall feedback survey should also be sent, asking:

- Did you feel this meeting was productive?
- Did you feel your concerns were heard?
- What topics would you like addressed in the next town hall?

This reinforces trust and accountability—employees will see that leadership is not just hosting town halls but actively working to improve communication and workplace fairness.

Virtual and Hybrid Adaptation: Making Two-Way Town Halls Work for Remote Teams

For remote-first or hybrid organizations, town halls should be designed with equal participation opportunities for virtual employees.

Ensuring Remote Employees Are Heard:

- Use a structured digital Q&A tool (such as Slido or a Teams/Slack thread) to collect questions in advance.
- Provide real-time chat functionality for live discussion.
- Assign a virtual moderator to monitor remote participation and ensure digital attendees are equally engaged.
- Record the session and make it accessible with time-stamped discussion points.

Virtual-Friendly Interactive Elements:

- Live polls and surveys during the session
- Breakout rooms for virtual discussions
- Anonymous feedback channels for post-event follow-up

A virtual-first mindset ensures that employees, regardless of location, have an equal seat at the table.

Why This Town Hall Structure Works:

- Ensures fairness—prevents the loudest voices from dominating.
- Encourages real participation—engages in-person and remote employees equally.
- Provides structure while allowing flexibility—keeps discussions on track but open to employee input.
- Strengthens leadership credibility—demonstrates active listening and accountability.
- Turns employee feedback into measurable action—ensures real impact beyond the meeting.

Implementing Two-Way Town Halls as an Ongoing Practice:

To embed this into company culture:

- Commit to a consistent town hall schedule.
- Measure engagement trends over time.
- Regularly refine the process based on employee feedback.

By prioritizing structured, transparent communication, leadership can bridge the gap between decision makers and employees, fostering a workplace culture where every voice is heard and valued.

The 360° Leadership Lab: Applying Fairness, Kindness, and Structure in Real Time

A Comprehensive Exercise to Strengthen Leadership Decision Making Across All Three Pillars

Objective:

- Provide leaders with a real-world, high-stakes decision-making scenario where they must apply *fairness*, *kindness*, and *structure* simultaneously.
- Help teams recognize the trade-offs between different leadership approaches and identify gaps in their decision-making habits.
- Encourage collaborative problem-solving that works in both small and large organizations, virtual or in person.

Step 1—Setting the Challenge (5 Minutes):

Participants are divided into small groups (3–5 people). Each group plays the role of a leadership team responsible for solving a workplace challenge.

Scenario Options (Facilitator Chooses One or Groups Pick at Random):

- A major budget cut forces leadership to choose between laying off employees or reducing benefits across the board.
- A highly valued employee is accused of unethical behavior. How do you handle transparency, fairness, and team morale?
- A restructuring plan is introduced, but employees feel left out of the decision-making process. How do you regain trust?
- A remote versus in-office policy conflict arises—some employees feel remote workers are treated unfairly.

Each group is tasked with finding a solution that balances:

- Fairness (Is the solution equitable for all employees?)
- Kindness (How does leadership demonstrate empathy while maintaining professionalism?)
- Structure (How will leadership communicate and enforce the decision effectively?)

Step 2—Decision Making in Action (20 Minutes, Group Work):

Each group must make and justify a final decision using this framework:

1. Fairness Assessment:
   - How does this decision impact different employee groups?
   - Are we applying consistent standards?
   - How will we ensure fairness is seen and understood?
2. Kindness Consideration:
   - How do we communicate this decision with empathy?
   - What support systems will we put in place for affected employees?
   - How do we balance business needs with human impact?
3. Structured Implementation:
   - How will the decision be announced (town hall, memo, personal meetings)?
   - How will leadership handle pushback and questions?
   - What next steps and accountability measures will be included?

Each group documents their decision and process in a structured format.

Step 3—The Leadership Cross-Examination (20 Minutes, Group Presentations):

Each group presents their decision as if they were leadership facing a board of employees.

- Other groups act as employees—asking challenging questions about the decision.
- The presenting group must defend their approach while staying within the Fairness-Kindness-Structure framework.

- Facilitator encourages constructive critique:
  - Did the decision feel fair?
  - Was kindness authentic or performative?
  - Could the structure be improved?

This stage replicates real-world leadership pressure, forcing teams to think beyond theory.

Step 4—The Reflection and Application (10 Minutes, Individual and Group Discussion):

Each participant reflects individually:

- Did we favor one pillar over the others?
- In real life, where do we struggle most as leaders—Fairness, Kindness, or Structure?
- What is one change we can make in our leadership approach based on this exercise?

Small groups reconvene to discuss lessons learned and real-world applications.

Version	In-Person	Virtual
Group Work	Small teams discuss in a room.	Breakout rooms on Zoom or Teams.
Decision Documentation	Flip charts, sticky notes, or whiteboards.	Shared Google Docs or Miro boards.
Cross-Examination	Present in front of the room, others ask questions live.	Each team presents in the main Zoom/Teams room, others respond via chat or live mic.
Final Reflection	Journaling, then group discussion.	Short survey, then discussion in the chat or breakout groups.

Figure 6: The Toolbox (360 Challenge)

Why This Works:

- Brings all three pillars together in a high-stakes scenario, ensuring leaders don't just focus on one area.

- Encourages real-world application—leaders practice responding to challenges under pressure.
- Promotes collaborative leadership—teams work through disagreements and find balanced solutions.
- Adapts easily to any workplace—can be used with executive teams, managers, or even students learning leadership skills.

This exercise helps participants see leadership from multiple angles, ensuring they leave with practical strategies for balancing Fairness, Kindness, and Structure in their own leadership roles.

For The Skeptics

(Or, "I Get It, I Think This Is Fluff")

If you've made it this far and you're still skeptical about Engaged Empathy Leadership Model (EELM), I respect that. Leadership books are notorious for grand theories that sound great on paper but fall apart in the real world. Maybe you're thinking, *This would never work in my organization*, or, *This is just another trendy leadership philosophy that will fade.*

But here's the thing: EELM isn't a gimmick. It's not a TED Talk buzzword, an HR fad, or a feel-good initiative designed to make employees happy while sacrificing business outcomes. It's a research-backed approach designed to solve real leadership problems—problems you're probably already dealing with.

So let's tackle some of the biggest pushbacks head-on.

Pushback #1: "What If My Organization Is Too Big for This?"

Translation: This all sounds great for startups and small businesses, but I work in a large, complex organization. There's no way we can implement this at scale.

The Truth: Size Doesn't Kill Leadership—Bureaucracy Does

Yes, large organizations have layers of management, red tape, and competing priorities. But your employees still crave fairness, structure, and engagement. In fact, big organizations need EELM more than anyone because bureaucracy often creates confusion, disengagement, and leadership blind spots.

Solution: Implement EELM at a Leadership Level First

- You don't need every department to flip overnight. Start with midlevel managers and ensure they're using structured feedback, transparent promotions, and engagement strategies.
- Use quarterly town halls or structured feedback loops to ensure employees feel heard, even in large companies.
- Research shows that engagement scales best when implemented at the leadership level first—if leaders model it, employees follow.

Research-Backed Fact:

A Gallup study found that companies with over 1,000 employees who implemented structured leadership engagement strategies saw a 21 percent increase in profitability and a 17 percent rise in productivity.

The Real Question:

Is your company too big for EELM, or is it too stuck in outdated leadership models to evolve?

Pushback #2: "What If My Employees Don't Respond to Empathy?"

Translation: Look, I work in an industry where people don't care about warm and fuzzy leadership. My employees want results, not feelings.

Reality Check: Empathy Isn't a Group Hug—It's a Strategy

Let's be clear: EELM is not about coddling employees. It's about engagement, retention, and performance.

- Empathy isn't about excusing poor performance. It's about understanding what motivates employees and using that knowledge to drive results.
- You don't need to be everyone's best friend—you just need to communicate clearly, recognize effort, and treat people fairly.

Solution:

- If you lead a high-pressure, results-driven team, structure is your empathy. Employees don't need you to hold their hand—they need clear expectations, transparent decision making, and fair performance reviews.
- Use direct but constructive feedback—research shows that leaders who provide structured, honest communication while acknowledging employee contributions increase performance by up to 30 percent.
- Empathy doesn't mean lowering standards. It means removing the roadblocks that prevent employees from meeting them.

Research-Backed Fact:

A *Harvard Business Review* study found that teams with empathetic leadership outperformed those without it by 20 percent in productivity. Why? Because employees who feel respected and valued work harder.

The Real Question:

Do your employees not respond to empathy, or have they just never experienced empathy paired with accountability and structure?

Pushback #3: "What If I Don't Have Time to Build Structure?"

Translation: I'm already overloaded. I don't have time to implement new leadership strategies—I barely have time to do my actual job.

Reality Check: If You're Too Busy for Structure, You're Too Busy to Lead

I get it. Leadership is demanding. But here's the irony—the more unstructured your leadership is, the more chaotic your team becomes. And chaos wastes more time than structure ever will.

- Lack of clarity leads to constant interruptions. Employees who don't know what's expected of them come to you for answers repeatedly.
- Confusion slows down decision making. If employees aren't sure how things work, they spend more time guessing, waiting for approval, or fixing mistakes.
- High turnover creates more work for you. If employees leave because of bad leadership, guess who has to train the replacements?

Solution:

- Start small. Implement one structured leadership habit at a time—whether it's quarterly check-ins, town halls, or structured promotion criteria.
- Batch your leadership efforts. Instead of reacting to problems daily, set dedicated time for structured engagement so you're not constantly putting out fires.
- Use delegation as structure. If your workload is overwhelming, build a leadership pipeline where team leads handle structured engagement, freeing up your time.

Research-Backed Fact:

A McKinsey study found that organizations with structured leadership models saved an average of 6 hours per manager per week because employees had clearer expectations, reducing the need for constant course correction.

The Real Question:

Do you really not have time for structure, or are you spending time managing the inefficiencies that a lack of structure creates?

The Cost of Ignoring Leadership Evolution

If you're skeptical of Engaged Empathy Leadership Model (EELM), I get it—change is uncomfortable.

But you know what else is uncomfortable?

- High turnover. Watching talented employees walk out the door because they don't see a future in your organization.
- Disengagement. Seeing a team that's just going through the motions, doing the bare minimum, and mentally checking out.
- Constantly putting out fires. Fixing problems that could have been prevented with better leadership, having the same conversations over and over, and scrambling to cover gaps left by burned-out employees.
- Replacing people over and over. Hiring, onboarding, and training new employees just to lose them 6 months later while your remaining team carries the extra weight.

That's not leadership. That's survival.

EELM: The Leadership Model That Lasts

At the end of the day, you don't have to choose between engagement and results. You don't have to pick between fairness and efficiency. You don't have to decide whether you want a kind workplace or a productive one.

The best leaders do both.

- They create structure without rigidity.
- They set expectations without micromanaging.
- They hold people accountable without making them feel like cogs in a machine.

And the organizations that thrive?

They're not the ones clinging to outdated leadership styles because "that's how it's always been done."

They're not the ones ignoring disengagement because "that's just how employees are these days."

They're the ones that stop making excuses and start leading better.

Because here's the real truth: EELM isn't just a nice idea. It's the difference between leading a workforce that blooms and one that withers.

The Research Behind the Engaged Empathy Leadership Model (EELM)

Expanding the Research: The Foundations of Engaged Empathy Leadership Model (EELM)

Leadership is not a one-size-fits-all concept, and over the years, various frameworks have shaped how organizations approach leadership development. The Engaged Empathy Leadership Model (EELM) builds upon existing theories while offering a unique structure that combines empathy, fairness, and structured leadership. This section will explore the research behind EELM and compare it to widely recognized leadership frameworks to highlight what makes it distinctive.

Research Insights: What Employees Want from Leadership

The development of EELM was rooted in firsthand research, combining survey data, in-depth interviews, and real-world case studies. My research, which surveyed 250 Gen Z employees across multiple industries, revealed a consistent expectation: employees want leadership that is not just empathetic but actively engaged in supporting their growth, success, and workplace experience.

Key Findings from the Research:

1. Employees Want Fairness and Transparency
   - Ninety-two percent of Gen Z employees ranked fairness in leadership decisions as the most critical factor in their workplace engagement.

- ○ Employees who felt promotions, performance reviews, and compensation were clearly explained and equitably distributed were significantly more likely to stay with their employer.

2. Structure and Clarity Drive Engagement
   - ○ Eighty-seven percent of Gen Z employees stated that they prefer clear career roadmaps and structured feedback over undefined flexibility.
   - ○ While work–life balance is important, employees reported higher engagement in workplaces with clear expectations and documented growth paths.

3. Empathy Alone Is Not Enough
   - ○ Eighty-five percent of employees reported that empathetic leadership improves workplace satisfaction, but they also noted that without fairness and structured leadership, empathy loses its impact.
   - ○ Employees need leaders who act on their empathy, ensuring that policies, promotions, and feedback processes reflect their stated values.

The EELM Advantage: Addressing Leadership Gaps

While many leadership models emphasize empathy, emotional intelligence, or structure individually, few integrate all three in a way that balances engagement with business outcomes. EELM fills this gap by offering a structured, action-driven approach to engaged leadership rather than relying on passive understanding or hierarchical control.

Comparing EELM to Established Leadership Frameworks

Transformational Leadership Versus EELM

Transformational leadership emphasizes visionary leadership, motivation, and inspiring employees to exceed expectations. Leaders who adopt this approach focus on charisma, intellectual stimulation, and individualized consideration.

Transformational Leadership	EELM™
Focuses on inspiring and motivating employees toward a shared vision.	Focuses on day-to-day engagement, fairness, and structured leadership.
Encourages leaders to act as role models.	Encourages leaders to act as mentors and transparent decision makers.
Can rely heavily on charismatic leadership that not all managers possess.	Does not require charisma—relies on repeatable, structured leadership actions.
May lack a structured approach to employee growth pathways.	Provides structured feedback loops and clear career progression.

Figure 7: Insights from the Research: What Employees Want from Leadership

While transformational leadership is effective in driving motivation and inspiring change, it sometimes lacks the structured processes needed for employees to see tangible career growth. EELM ensures that leadership isn't just inspirational—it's actionable and sustainable.

Servant Leadership Versus EELM

Servant leadership is built on the philosophy that leaders should serve their teams first, prioritizing the needs of employees before their own. This approach promotes empathy, listening, and collaboration.

Servant Leadership	EELM™
Focuses on putting employees' needs first and fostering a strong culture of support.	Focuses on balancing empathy with structured leadership to ensure fairness and business results.
Encourages leaders to act as servants to their teams.	Encourages leaders to act as partners in engagement, providing clear guidance while supporting employees.
Can create leadership burnout if leaders overextend themselves.	Prevents burnout by ensuring leaders maintain authority and structure.
Sometimes lacks clear guidelines on accountability and expectations.	Establishes structured feedback systems to keep both leaders and employees accountable.

Figure 8: Insights from the Research: What Employees Want from Leadership

While servant leadership is effective in building trust and fostering a sense of community it sometimes lacks the structural foundation needed for clear decision making and business-driven leadership. EELM takes the best aspects of servant leadership—empathy and engagement—and pairs them with structured decision making and fairness.

Transactional Leadership Versus EELM

Transactional Leadership is based on rules, performance-based rewards, and clear expectations. Leaders focus on efficiency, standardization, and structured decision making.

Transactional Leadership	EELM™
Focuses on strict hierarchy, rules, and reward systems.	Provides clear structure without rigidity, balancing accountability with flexibility.
Employees receive rewards or punishments based on performance metrics.	Employees receive fair, structured feedback and transparent career paths.
Lacks empathy—prioritizes efficiency over engagement.	Prioritizes engagement without sacrificing structure and business goals.
Can feel rigid, bureaucratic, and outdated for modern employees.	Appeals to modern employees (especially Gen Z) by integrating structure with fairness and engagement.

Figure 9: Insights from the Research: What Employees Want from Leadership

Why EELM Stands Out

Unlike traditional leadership models, EELM is built specifically for the modern workforce. It acknowledges that empathy alone doesn't drive results, structure alone doesn't engage employees, and fairness alone doesn't ensure long-term success.

EELM blends the best aspects of other leadership models while addressing their shortcomings:

- Like Transformational Leadership, it fosters employee motivation—but with structured career paths and fairness built in.
- Like Servant Leadership, it emphasizes employee engagement—but ensures leaders maintain authority, structure, and clarity.
- Like Transactional Leadership, it values clear expectations and accountability—but without rigidity or outdated hierarchical thinking.

The Leadership Model for the Future

Leadership is evolving. Employees—especially Gen Z—expect leaders who engage, communicate, and provide structure without micromanaging. They are no longer willing to work under leaders who rely on passive empathy without action, fairness without transparency, or structure without flexibility.

The Engaged Empathy Leadership Model provides a clear, actionable framework for modern leaders to develop teams that are not just productive but engaged, motivated, and built to last.

Organizations that integrate EELM into their leadership philosophy won't just retain top talent—they'll create thriving workplaces that stand the test of time.

Leading Across Generations with EELM

EELM provides a leadership framework that can be customized based on generational needs, ensuring that all employees feel engaged, valued, and supported.

Baby Boomers (Boomers) (1946–1964)—Experience Driven and Structure Oriented:

- Boomers respect clear hierarchies and structure. They grew up in traditional workplace environments where longevity and loyalty were rewarded.
- They value stability and experience. Many boomers have spent decades in their industries and expect recognition for their expertise.
- How EELM Applies:
  - Provide structured feedback and clear advancement pathways to keep Boomers engaged in leadership roles.
  - Recognize their contributions through mentorship opportunities, advisory roles, and strategic decision-making positions.

Generation X (Gen X) (1965–1980) —Independent but Fairness Oriented:

- Gen X prefers autonomy—they grew up in an era of self-sufficiency and skepticism toward authority.

- They value work–life balance and fairness but tend to be less vocal than millennials and Gen Z about workplace concerns.
- How EELM Applies:
  - Allow for autonomous leadership styles but maintain clear company expectations and transparent decision making.
  - Ensure fair promotion structures—Gen X employees will leave if they feel overlooked for younger talent.
  - Encourage direct but structured communication—Gen X appreciates leadership that is straightforward and solutions focused.

Millennials (1981–1996)—Purpose Driven and Engagement Oriented:

- Millennials prioritize purpose, values, and professional development. They need leaders who connect their work to a broader mission.
- They value collaboration and fairness. Unlike Gen X, millennials tend to voice their expectations openly and expect leadership to listen and respond.
- How EELM Applies:
  - Leaders should tie work to meaningful impact—millennials thrive in workplaces where they feel their contributions matter beyond profit.
  - Use structured town halls and feedback loops to keep millennials engaged in decision making.
  - Ensure fairness in pay transparency, career growth, and leadership opportunities—millennials expect clear, structured paths to success.

Generation Z (1997–2012)—Transparency and Structure Oriented:

- Gen Z expects immediate clarity. Unlike millennials, they don't just want purpose—they also demand structure and fairness.
- They value leadership that is direct, open, and engaged. They won't hesitate to leave if an organization fails to provide transparency.
- How EELM Applies:
  - Provide structured career paths with clear expectations from day one.

- Ensure open communication through regular town halls, check-ins, and mentorship programs.
- Use real-time feedback loops—Gen Z doesn't want to wait months for performance discussions.

Study 1: Workplace Environment and Leadership Preferences of Generation Z

Research Overview:

My doctoral dissertation examined how workplace environments and leadership styles impact Gen Z engagement, retention, and job satisfaction. This study was based on Kahn's Employee Engagement Theory, which suggests that personal role engagement is influenced by psychological safety, meaningful work, and resource availability.

Methodology:

- Research Type: Qualitative multiple case study
- Participants:
    - Ten Gen Z employees (ages 18–21, with at least 1 year of work experience)
    - Ten employers (business owners or managers with at least two Gen Z employees)
- Data Collection:
    - Semistructured, one-on-one interviews with both employees and employers
    - Open-ended questions on workplace environment, leadership expectations, and engagement drivers
    - Thematic analysis to identify leadership patterns

Key Findings:

- **Fairness, structure, and kindness drive engagement.** Gen Z employees highly value transparent decision making, structured growth opportunities, and leadership that is both supportive and accountable. Organizations that provide clear guidelines and career paths see significantly higher engagement.

- **Workplace environment impacts performance and retention.** Employees working in structured, well-organized environments reported higher motivation and job satisfaction. Chaotic, disorganized, or toxic workplaces led to frustration and high turnover.
- **Gen Z employees seek growth and clarity.** Unclear career paths and lack of leadership development were the top reasons employees considered leaving a company. Growth wasn't just about promotions—employees valued mentorship, skill development, and opportunities for leadership roles.
- **Supervisor behavior directly affects employee engagement.** Employees consistently linked their workplace mood, motivation, and performance to their direct supervisor's leadership style. Regular, structured feedback increased engagement, while a lack of supervisor involvement led to turnover.
- **Transformational leadership is preferred.** Transformational leaders, who focus on mentorship and inspiration, were favored over transactional, top-down, or hands-off leaders. Employees responded best to leaders who led by example, actively participated in problem-solving, and engaged in regular communication.

Implications for Organizations:

Companies that want to attract and retain Gen Z talent need to prioritize fairness, structured career growth, and engaged leadership. Leaders must balance empathy with action, providing both emotional intelligence and structured accountability. Workplace culture must be intentionally shaped, as disorganized or toxic environments can quickly drive Gen Z employees away. Mentorship and leadership development programs should be formalized, offering clear pathways for advancement.

Study 2: Generation Z Workplace Survey (250 Participants)

Research Overview:

This study aimed to measure the leadership behaviors that most impact Gen Z engagement, retention, and job satisfaction.

Methodology:

- Survey Distribution: Conducted via e-mail, in-person sessions, and social media
- Participants: 250 Gen Z employees across technology, hospitality, education, and manufacturing industries
- Survey Focus Areas:
  - Leadership qualities that matter most
  - Workplace factors contributing to job satisfaction and retention
  - The impact of fairness, structure, and empathy in leadership

Key Findings:

- **Fairness is the top factor in retention**. Ninety-two percent of Gen Z employees ranked fairness as the most important leadership quality. Employees who perceived their workplace as fair were 67 percent more likely to stay long-term.
- **Structure drives engagement more than flexibility**. Eighty-seven percent of employees preferred structured performance reviews and defined career paths over informal evaluations. Employees in companies with clear role expectations reported higher engagement.
- **Empathy alone is not enough**. Eighty-five percent agreed that empathetic leadership improves workplace culture, but without fairness and structured feedback, empathy feels hollow. Employees expect leaders to act on their concerns, not just acknowledge them.

Implications for Organizations:

Organizations that integrate transparent decision making, structured career growth, and engaged leadership models will attract and retain top talent.

Study 3: The 175-Person Leadership Expectations Survey

Research Overview:

This survey examined what leadership qualities Gen Z expects in the workplace.

Methodology:

- Participants: 175 Gen Z respondents (ages 18–21)
- Survey Focus Areas:
  - Ranking the top leadership traits expected from employers
  - Identifying factors contributing to workplace engagement

Top Leadership Qualities Gen Z Expects:

1. Organization—Clear job expectations and structured leadership
2. Respect—Fair treatment and value of individual input
3. Communication—Open, honest leadership
4. Positive Attitude—Supportive, motivating managers
5. Approachability—Leaders whom employees feel comfortable talking to
6. Flexibility—Some autonomy in work schedules
7. Fair Pay—Transparent and equitable salaries
8. Responsibility—Leaders who take accountability
9. Trust—Confidence in leadership decision making
10. Acknowledgment—Regular recognition of employee contributions

Implications for Organizations:

Gen Z expects structured, engaged, and transparent leadership. Passive or ambiguous leadership styles do not resonate with this workforce.

Works Cited

Books and Academic Research

Bass, Bernard M. 1985. *Leadership and Performance Beyond Expectations*. Free Press.

Buckingham, Marcus, and Ashley Goodall. 2019. *Nine Lies About Work: A Freethinking Leader's Guide to the Real World*. Harvard Business Review Press.

Dweck, C.S. 2006. *Mindset: The New Psychology of Success*. Random House Publishing Group.

Edmondson, Amy C. 2019. *The Fearless Organization: Creating Psychological Safety in the Workplace for Learning, Innovation, and Growth*. Wiley.

Goleman, Daniel. 1998. *Working with Emotional Intelligence*. Bantam Books.

Kahn, William A. 1990. "Psychological Conditions of Personal Engagement and Disengagement at Work." *Academy of Management Journal* 33 (4): 692–724.

Kegan, Robert, and Lisa Laskow Lahey. 2016. *An Everyone Culture: Becoming a Deliberately Developmental Organization*. Harvard Business Review Press.

Kirchmayer, Zuzana, and Jana Fratričová. 2020. "What Motivates Generation Z at Work? Insights into Motivation Drivers of Business Students in Slovakia." *Journal of Human Resource Management* 23 (2): 28–39.

LeBlanc, Jeff. 2022. *Workplace Environment and Leadership Preferences of Generation Z*. National University.

Smith, John R., Emily Carter, and Rachel Huang. 2020. "Empathetic Leadership and Employee Retention: A Meta-Analysis." *Journal of Applied Psychology* 105 (3): 245–262.

Industry Reports and Studies

DDI. 2019. *New DDI Research: 57 Percent of Employees Quit Because of Their Boss*. https://www.prnewswire.com/news-releases/new-ddi-research-57-percent-of-employees-quit-because-of-their-boss-300971506.html.

Gallup. 2017. *American Workplace Changing at a Dizzying Pace*. https://www.gallup.com/workplace/236282/american-workplace-changing-dizzying-pace.aspx.

Gallup. 2019. *Creating a Culture of Recognition*. Gallup, Inc. https://www.gallup.com/analytics/472658/workplace-recognition-research.aspx.

Gallup. 2021. *State of the American Workplace 2021 Report*. Gallup, Inc. https://bendchamber.org/wp-content/uploads/2021/12/state-of-the-global-workplace-2021-download.pdf.

Gallup. 2023. *What Gen Z Wants from Work and Leadership*. Gallup, Inc. https://www.gallup.com/workplace/610856/new-challenge-engaging-younger-workers.aspx.

Google. 2013. *Project Oxygen: What Makes a Great Manager?* Google People Operations Research Report. https://newageleadership.com/wp-content/uploads/2020/04/Project-Oxygen.pdf.

Harvard Business Review. 2016. "The Neuroscience of Trust." *Harvard Business Review*, November 2016. https://hbr.org/2017/01/the-neuroscience-of-trust.

Harvard Business Review. 2022. "Why Empathy Alone Isn't Enough for Effective Leadership." *Harvard Business Review*, June 2022. https://hbr.org/2023/.../empathetic-leadership-how-to-go-beyond-lip-service.

LinkedIn. 2022. *The Future of Recruiting: How Gen Z is Changing the Workforce.* LinkedIn Talent Solutions. https://business.linkedin.com/talent-solutions/resources/future-of-recruiting

McKinsey & Company. 2018. *How Leaders Listen: Closing the Leadership Perception Gap.* McKinsey & Company.

McKinsey & Company. 2022. *The State of the American Workforce: Engaging Gen Z Employees in a Post-Pandemic Economy.* McKinsey & Company.

SHRM (Society for Human Resource Management). 2023. *The Future of Leadership Development: How Organizations Can Adapt to a Multi-Generational Workforce.* SHRM Research Report. https://www.shrm.org/content/dam/en/shrm/about/Annual-Report-2023.pdf.

The Engagement Institute. 2017. *The Cost of Employee Disengagement.* A Collaboration of The Conference Board, Deloitte, and Sirota. https://www.hrdive.com/news/study-disengaged-employees-can-cost-companies-up-to-550b-a-year/437606/.

Surveys and Case Studies from the Engaged Empathy Leadership Model (EELM) Research

- LeBlanc, Jeff. 2024. *Generation Z Workplace Survey (250 Participants).* Unpublished survey data collected across technology, hospitality, education, and manufacturing industries.

- LeBlanc, Jeff. 2024. *Leadership Engagement Case Studies.* Data collected from organizations implementing EELM, including:
  - **Tutoring Company:** 18 percent increase in retention, 22 percent improvement in employee satisfaction after implementing casual one-on-one check-ins.
  - **Production Company:** 30 percent increase in interdepartmental collaboration after restructuring the bonus system to reward team outcomes.
  - **Hospitality Business:** 40 percent increase in career growth perceptions, 25 percent improvement in retention after implementing structured quarterly town halls.

About the Author

Dr. Jeff LeBlanc is a professor, leadership strategist, and award-winning educator specializing in business strategy, organizational behavior, and workplace engagement. He is the creator of the Engaged Empathy Leadership Model (EELM), a research-backed framework designed to help leaders balance kindness, fairness, and structure to foster high-performing, engaged teams.

Dr. LeBlanc holds degrees in communication, an MBA, and a doctorate in business administration (DBA) with a focus on organizational leadership. He has taught at Bentley University and other institutions, where he equips students and professionals with the tools to navigate the evolving workforce. His innovative teaching methods earned him Bentley University's Innovation in Teaching Award for his Gen Z-focused curriculum.

Beyond academia, Dr. LeBlanc has worked with businesses, startups, and industry leaders to implement structured, empathy-driven leadership practices that drive retention, performance, and workplace satisfaction. His insights have been featured in Fast Company, Boston Business Journal, and Black Enterprise, and he regularly speaks at corporate and academic events.

A passionate advocate for practical, research-based leadership development, Dr. LeBlanc's work bridges the gap between theory and application. His research on Gen Z leadership preferences and employee engagement has influenced how organizations adapt to the changing workforce.

Outside of teaching and consulting, he serves on the board of Haverhill Promise, a literacy initiative supporting young readers in his hometown of Haverhill, Massachusetts.

For more insights and resources, visit www.jeffleblancdba.com.

Index